VOLUNTEERS

The Betrayal of National Defense Secrets by Air Force Traitors

David J. Crawford

HQ Air Force Office of Special Investigations
Directorate of Counterintelligence
Bolling Air Force Base
Washington, D.C. 20332

MAY 1988

Volunteers

"It's not easy to recruit Americans. Money prompts many of them to find us. But look at it statistically. The US is a nation of 260 million people, only a tiny minority end up working for the Soviet Union. If people don't volunteer, it's very hard to recruit Americans. Getting a key American source automatically earns one the highest award in the Soviet Union, The Order of Lenin."

Stanislav Levchenko
Ex-KGB Major
Interview for Defense and Electronics Magazine

"I think that if I were asked to single out one specific group of men, one category, as being the most suspicious, unreasonable, petty, inhuman, sadistic, double-crossing, set of bastards in any language, I would say without hesitation: 'The people who run counterespionage departments.'"

Erick Ambler
The Light of Day

TABLE OF CONTENTS

	PAGE
ACKNOWLEDGMENTS	iii
FOREWARD	v
LIST OF ILLUSTRATIONS	ix
Chapter 1 INTRODUCTION	1
Chapter 2 RECRUITMENT AND THE VOLUNTEER	6
Chapter 3 CLANDESTINE COMMUNICATIONS	24
Chapter 4 PATTERNS AND TRENDS	60
Chapter 5 CASE SUMMARIES	84
AHADI*	86
BOECKENHAUPT	88
BORGER	91
BRONSON*	95
BUCHANAN	101
CASCIO	106
COOKE	107
CREST*	112
DAVIES	117
DECHAMPLAIN	119
FRENCH	124

* pseudonyms

i

Volunteers

    GRUNDEN 127

    HERMAN* 128

    JONES 131

    KAUFFMAN 132

    MIRA 139

    MUELLER 144

    OTT 146

    PERKINS 151

    THOMPSON 157

    WALTON* 162

    WESSON* 163

    WOOD 164

Chapter 6
CONCLUSIONS 169

Appendix 1
HOSTILE INTELLIGENCE THREAT 174

Appendix 2
ESPIONAGE ARRESTS AND PROSECUTIONS 187

Appendix 3
DOD PERSONNEL ARRESTED FOR ESPIONAGE 188

Appendix 4
MOTIVATION OF DOD PERSONNEL ARRESTED FOR ESPIONAGE 190

ENDNOTES 192

BIBLIOGRAPHY 208

ACKNOWLEDGMENTS

Treason is a crime, a public wrong, which attacks the very existence of the Government itself. Traitors betray not only their country, but their friends, families, and way of life. It is difficult to detect espionage, as well as to understand its causes. We have prepared this study to provide security officials, defense contractors, and the general public with insight into the nature of espionage directed against the United States Air Force.

I would like to thank the many people who were involved in making this project a success. First, the author, Captain Dave Crawford. As a student at the Defense Intelligence College, he submitted a classified Master's thesis entitled <u>Espionage in the Air Force Since World War II</u>. This thesis was selected as the outstanding research paper of the academic year and earned him the Defense Intelligence Research Award. Capt Crawford developed <u>Volunteers: The Betrayal of National Defense Secrets by Air Force Traitors</u> from his classified thesis.

Other AFOSI special agents who provided invaluable contributions to this text are: Brigadier General Richard Beyea, Richard Law, Charles Torpy, Scott Schrader, Wayne P. Hufnagel, Daniel J. Bruno, Stephen G. Gottrich, Earl Middaugh, Alan Huff, Richard Certo, Bruce Wimmer, Wally Holland, Robert Miglia, Paul Andrews, and Robert Gold. Craig Goheen, Hillary Kaplan, and Ronald Woodward of the Defense Intelligence College also significantly contributed to this project. The editors, Robin Misner Boatman and Pamela J. Dobson, spent many hours working with the text. Administrative support was provided by Janet Marek and Jasmine Salter; cover design and

Volunteers

graphic support, Adan Caraballo and Lisa Hennessey; and photographic support, Steve Hawkins. A special thanks to Linda Garmon, HQ USAF Publishing Division and Alice Kottmyer, HQ USAF Judge Advocate Office, who both worked diligently on this publication.

CHARLES F. JOHNSON, Colonel, USAF
Director of Counterintelligence
Air Force Office of Special Investigations

FOREWARD

The espionage efforts of hostile intelligence services (most notably those of the Soviet Union) have made U.S. Air Force (USAF) communications, weapons systems, wartime readiness plans, and policies vulnerable since the USAF was created as a separate armed service in 1947. This vulnerability has directly impacted on U.S. national security and resulted in thousands of dollars being spent to modify plans or improve communication and weapons systems which have been compromised. A comparative analysis and description of espionage activity involving all USAF personnel known to be involved in espionage, or attempting to engage in espionage, has never been previously prepared at the unclassified level, although some cases have been examined individually and several cases have been compared. This study is, therefore, the first complete descriptive analysis of all known espionage cases involving USAF personnel.

The perplexing problem of how hostile intelligence services engage in espionage operations directed against the USAF and what characteristics are commonly found among Air Force members who become involved in espionage are examined, as well as how and why they become involved and how they communicate clandestinely with the hostile intelligence service to betray our political and military defense secrets. The nature of espionage in the Air Force will be traced by examining 23 case histories of USAF traitors who either committed or attempted to commit espionage. Foreign national employees (local hire) and defense contractor employees are not included.

To consider only employees <u>convicted</u> of espionage or on active duty at the time of detection in a study of espionage

Volunteers

in the USAF would be closing one's mind to reality. In several cases there exists strong indication of involvement, intent, and damage to national security, despite the absence or overturning of a court conviction. In a few cases no attempt was made to prosecute because of lack of evidence or to protect sensitive sources and techniques.[*]

Additionally, some of the cases discussed were not detected until the person had separated from the USAF; yet, with the exception of two, there is little doubt that the suspect engaged in espionage prior to his release from active duty. All these cases are included because they have two commonalities: the individuals were involved in espionage activities with a foreign government, or were attempting to establish contact when detected; and they all served in the USAF on active duty, or were attached to the Department of the Air Force in a civilian capacity.

Although it would have been extremely beneficial for Air Force Office of Special Investigations (AFOSI) counterintelligence professionals, USAF security managers, and senior USAF leadership if specific characteristics could have been identified in this study which would be strongly

---

*Because of the Privacy Act of 1974, the names of six traitors cannot be disclosed because they were not prosecuted but administratively dismissed from the USAF under security regulations. Throughout this study these traitors will be referred to by pseudonyms. These pseudonyms are Ahadi, Bronson, Crest, Herman, Wesson, and Walton. Except for the pseudonym, all other information concerning these cases has not been changed.

Foreward

predictive that a USAF member may become involved in espionage--the unfortunate reality is that no such characteristics or "spy profile" exists that can be used to predict involvement. Although there are certain common factors in many of these espionage investigations, the counterintelligence officer must evaluate each allegation on its own merit. As will be described in this report, contrary to popular belief, traitors in the USAF have come from all walks of life and backgrounds, and in the majority of cases have **volunteered** to betray their country to a hostile intelligence service for monetary reasons. In most cases, USAF spies were not "recruited" (in the true meaning of the word) through a lengthy social cultivation process, nor were there many suspects who could be accurately described as "loners." These are two popular myths which have existed for many years, but hopefully they can be laid to rest. Although a predictive spy profile or list of definitive indicators does not exist, counterintelligence investigators may use the characteristics of suspects, as well as the patterns and trends described in this report as a guide when tasked to investigate a new espionage allegation.

This study is about traitors in the USAF. A <u>traitor</u> is a citizen of our country who betrays information to a foreign power. A <u>spy</u>, however, is a citizen of a foreign power who attempts to obtain information about our country.* The Soviet Union has little respect or sympathy for traitors and

---

*Admittedly, this pure definition is rarely used or understood. Today, a spy is considered to be anyone who acquires sensitive information and provides that information to a foreign power. Therefore, a spy may also be a traitor.

will abandon them when they are caught or become useless. In contrast, the Soviets will go to great lengths to bring back their own citizens or intelligence officers who have been arrested and imprisoned in the West.

Finally, to put espionage in the Air Force in the proper perspective, the reader must keep in mind that since World War II, millions of loyal Americans have served honorably in the Air Force. In terms of espionage, only 23 traitors can be found, statistically an insignificant number. Unfortunately, although there are few who would betray their country, those few who do can wreck havoc on the security of the United States and the Air Force.

ILLUSTRATIONS

	PAGE
1. Recruitment and Motivation	10
2. Sketch of Rollover Camera	44
3. Rollover Camera	45
4. Clandestine Instructions on Cellophane	46
5. Items in Typical Soviet (GRU) Dead Drop	47
6. Herbert Boeckenhaupt	48
7. Raymond DeChamplain	48
8. Christopher Cooke	49
9. Guisseppe Cascio	50
10. Gustav Mueller	51
11. Mr. and Mrs. George French	52
12. Captain George French	53
13. Patrick Kauffman	53
14. Bruce Ott	54
15. Walter Perkins	54
16. James Woods (pre-arrest)	55
17. James Woods (post-arrest)	55
18. Robert Thompson (pre-imprisonment)	56
19. Robert Thompson (imprisoned)	56
20. KGB Officer Malinin	57
21. KGB Officer Chernyestev	58
22. EGIS Officer (2Lt) Gunter Maennel	58
23. GRU Colonel Izmaylov	59
24. Age When Espionage Began	67
25. Years of Federal Service When Uncovered	68
26. Foreign Influence	70
27. Career Field of Traitors	72
28. Educational Backgrounds	76
29. Monies Received by USAF Traitors	78
30. Examples of Monies Received by Non-USAF Traitors	80
31. Christopher Cooke (post-arrest)	85
32. Capt George French	125
33. TSgt Walter Perkins	151

Chapter 1

INTRODUCTION

Since the conclusion of World War II and the creation of the United States Air Force (USAF) as a separate service under the National Security Act of 1947, 23 USAF military members and Department of the Air Force (DAF) civilian employees have been identified committing espionage on behalf of a foreign government or were thwarted in such attempts. Not all of these cases have been highly publicized and in some instances they were not disclosed to the public. In each case where the USAF member or DAF civilian employee was in actual contact with the foreign intelligence service, it is believed that classified information was provided which damaged the security of the Air Force and the Nation. In the remainder, such damage would have occurred if the espionage agent had not been detected and neutralized by proactive counterespionage investigations.

Espionage is without question one of the oldest professions known to man. Sun Tzu, an ancient Chinese warrior-philosopher (C. 500 B.C.) described in his book, <u>The Art of War</u>, the importance of good intelligence and how to obtain it through espionage:[1]

> Now the reason the enlightened prince and wise general conquer the enemy whenever they move and their achievements surpass those of ordinary men is foreknowledge.

Sun Tzu goes on to stress the importance of counterespionage when he says that:[2]

> It is essential to seek out enemy agents who have come to conduct espionage against you.....

Volunteers

Methods employed by intelligence services to "run" espionage agents can also be traced historically. In general, most people, including spies, have a basic instinct for survival. To be an effective espionage agent, one must acquire information and transmit that information to the intelligence service which he or she is spying for; but this task must be accomplished safely, if the spy is to continue undetected. To ensure the safety of the spy, and more importantly the operation, a unique set of principles (tradecraft) has been devised to run espionage agents.

The first "safe house" existed during biblical days when Joshua brought the Israeli force to within striking distance of Jericho and sent spies into the city where they remained in the house of Rahab, a prostitute, until making their escape.[3] In a more contemporary context, the American Continental Congress established the Committee of Secret Correspondence in November 1775, and this first U.S. intelligence service used a considerable amount of tradecraft. They employed codes and ciphers, chemical secret writing, and letter drops in communications between the Committee and its agents abroad.[4] The principles of espionage tradecraft have basically stayed the same for thousands of years. The only change has been in the use of modern technology in the development of clandestine communications. For example, the Nazis improved upon microdot technology during World War II;[5] the Soviets have used long-range radio communications with their agents around the world since at least the 1930's,[6] and today the Soviet

Introduction

intelligence services communicate with their agents via satellites.[7] USAF personnel who have become involved in espionage have used secret writing, dead drops, one-time pads, and a variety of other clandestine techniques for communicating with a hostile intelligence service.

The Air Force is a high-priority target of hostile intelligence services. Its personnel have been used as espionage agents almost since the establishment of the USAF as a separate service. The Soviet and Warsaw Pact intelligence services have concentrated on the USAF because of its level of industrial and weapons development, research, and technological innovation which offer a rich field for technologically inferior countries attempting to improve their own weapons research and development programs. Therefore, these countries desperately require scientific and technological information. Espionage against the USAF has caused serious damage to our war-fighting capability and has, at times, made the USAF extremely vulnerable. This vulnerability occurs because, until a traitor is detected, our enemies possess knowledge which we believe to be unknown to them. The USAF develops plans and assessments in the belief that capabilities, weaknesses, and true intentions are unknown to foreign powers and a traitor can easily undermine, exploit, or neutralize our security if he or she is compromising information to a hostile intelligence service.

Since the USAF was established, counterintelligence specialists have attempted to devise ways of identifying those individuals who are or who may become a traitor.

Volunteers

Although traitors come from a multitude of backgrounds and experiences, a general belief (or hope) has existed that a common factor, or group of factors, could be developed which would allow counterintelligence investigators to detect potential and actual traitors.

The main focus of this study is to review and analyze known cases of espionage or attempted espionage by USAF personnel and explore the nature of espionage in the USAF to determine if there are any common characteristics or factors which could be exploited by counterintelligence personnel to identify and neutralize espionage agents in the USAF. However, the major conclusion of this study is that there is no definitive and predictive profile of potential or actual USAF traitors. This study is unique in that all known subject USAF espionage cases (uncovered to date) have been accurately discussed, summarized, and analyzed at the unclassified level.* For the first time, counterintelligence officials, security managers, senior Air Force leaders, and the general public will be able to fully appreciate and understand the motivations and characteristics of those who have betrayed the Air Force and our country.

---

*Some material must remain classified, particularly information pertaining to investigative methods, techniques, sources, information provided by other countries or agencies, and information derived from cases which have yet to be prosecuted.

Introduction

Not only is this a review of espionage in the U.S. Air Force, it also provides interesting insight into an instrument of Soviet foreign policy which is often overlooked by many researchers--the impact of espionage. The reader will quickly discern that this report is primarily an overview of Soviet espionage efforts directed against the USAF and the United States because most cases deal with operations conducted by the Glavnoye Razvedyvatelnoye Upravleniye (GRU, or more commonly referred to as "military intelligence") and the Komitet Gosudarstvennoy Bezopasnosti (KGB).* With the exception of three cases, all others detailed in this study involved the GRU and the KGB. Throughout recent history, the Soviet Union has openly engaged the United States in negotiations; detente; and a quest for nuclear arms reductions and world peace, while at the same time aggressively seeking to locate, recruit, and "run" espionage agents, or to exploit the opportunities presented by volunteer traitors.

The following chapters will provide the reader with a brief but accurate description of espionage in the Air Force, as well as the tradecraft used by hostile intelligence services to penetrate the security of the United States.

---

*See Appendix 1 for a brief overview of the threat posed by the Soviet Intelligence Services (SIS).

Chapter 2

RECRUITMENT AND THE VOLUNTEER

> "Spies, being human, often invent a better-sounding motive if their sole reason for betraying their country is money."
>
> General Frantisek Moravec,
>   former head of Czechoslovakian Military Intelligence

The means and methods employed by hostile intelligence services to spot, vet, recruit,* and handle ("run") espionage agents are many and varied. Historically, espionage investigations have shown that Air Force traitors came from a wide range of individual backgrounds, but possessed two similar characteristics. First, the overwhelming majority of USAF individuals who betrayed their country through espionage have been volunteers--they have not been recruited in the usual meaning of the word. They made the spotting, vetting, and recruitment process easier by bringing themselves to the attention of the hostile intelligence service. The second similar characteristic is that either financial problems or outright greed was the motivating factor in almost every case, and a powerful secondary factor in most of the remaining. To fully comprehend espionage directed against the Air Force, it is important to understand the agent recruitment

---

*The word "recruitment" may either refer to the entire process or cycle (spotting, vetting, recruitment, training, and handling) or may refer to the actual stage when the espionage agent is "recruited." Although these stages are discussed in a specific order, they do not necessarily occur in this order in each recruitment, as will be explained in this chapter.

Recruitment and the Volunteer

process and how Air Force personnel historically have become involved in espionage.

For the hostile intelligence services to be successful in penetrating the Air Force and meeting their intelligence information collection requirements, they must exploit human sources (traitors) to acquire information which cannot be obtained through technical means of collection. More importantly, the human source can often provide the <u>true intentions</u> of Air Force and National leaders--which a technical collection system cannot. Additionally, technical systems can be deceived quite easily, but it is more difficult to deceive a human source who is collecting sensitive documents which can be reviewed, analyzed, and compared with other documents and information for confirmation. The Soviets, in particular, are more apt to believe information which they can acquire through espionage agents versus through technical collection. This explains their heavy use and emphasis of conducting clandestine human source operations against the United States.

Spotting is usually the first step in the recruitment cycle, and intelligence officers will go to great lengths to locate and identify suitable individuals to be their espionage agent. Obviously, people who travel to the Soviet Union or any other Warsaw Pact country, come to the attention of authorities before their arrival, often because they must have the necessary travel documents (passports, visas, and so forth) approved in advance by security officials. If anyone enters the country and is of interest, it is not very difficult for the Second Chief Directorate (Internal Security)

Volunteers

of the KGB to target and exploit opportunities for espionage recruitment. Warsaw Pact countries and other Soviet allies, such as Cuba, have modeled their intelligence services along Soviet lines and they all have a comparable Directorate which provides internal security and functions in the same manner as the Second Chief Directorate. Blackmail, coercion, entrapment, and frameups have been well documented by counterintelligence officials in the West and described in detail by authors such as Barron, Pincher, West, Deacon, Corson, and Crowley. Suffice it to say that, inside a totalitarian country, blackmail and coercion are valid techniques which can be used in the recruitment process, but when examining known cases of espionage among Air Force personnel, these tactics have been of little or no importance.

Outside the borders of the Soviet Union and their allies, spotting becomes more difficult for the intelligence service. In the KGB, the First Chief Directorate is responsible for espionage operations and similar departments exist in the intelligence structures of countries allied with the Soviet Union. In addition to the First Chief Directorate, the Soviet Union (and allies) employ the services of military intelligence officers, some of which are assigned as military attaches and others who are assigned in "cover" positions within the Soviet diplomatic, business, and journalist organizations found in most western countries. Military officers of Soviet allied countries are organized and operate in a similar fashion as their GRU counterparts.

The efforts of all of these intelligence officers are directed towards one objective--the identification and recruitment of espionage agents. Hostile intelligence officers working under their diplomatic cover visit restaurants, bars, discos, amusement parks, and shopping malls, seeking a chance encounter which can be exploited. They join business clubs, social groups, and attend public meetings, hoping for exploitable opportunities. Simply, they take advantage of the freedoms developed in western democracies to spot suitable espionage agents. Of more importance, is the fact that in a democratic country, the opportunity to volunteer to commit espionage is easier if any individual chooses to do so, and volunteers have proven to be lucrative espionage agents for the Soviets.

Although the KGB and GRU will recruit individuals with problems (homosexuality, drug abuse, alcoholism, and so forth) these traitors are difficult to control and handle. Obviously, they would prefer to recruit happily married, respected members of the community who keep a low profile. This reduces the likelihood that the operation will be compromised.

As can be seen from Figure 1, the majority of USAF traitors who have become involved in espionage were volunteers, primarily motivated by money. In a few cases, the traitor claimed to have been coerced (**Thompson, DeChamplain, and Kauffman**), but there is little or no evidence to support their claims. In another case (**Perkins**), coercion is also claimed, but the evidence is contradictory at best.

Figure 1

RECRUITMENT AND MOTIVATION

Name	Recruitment	Motivation
Ahadi*	Volunteer	Ideological
Boeckenhaupt	Volunteer	Money
Borger	Volunteer	Money
Bronson*	Volunteer	Money
Buchanan	Volunteer	Money
Cascio	Volunteer	Money
Cooke	Volunteer	Ego/Adventure
Crest*	Recruited	Money
Davies	Volunteer	Disaffection/Revenge
DeChamplain	Volunteer	Money
French	Volunteer	Money
Grunden	Volunteer	Money
Herman*	Unknown	Money
Kauffman	Volunteer	Disaffection
Jones	Volunteer	Money
Mira	Volunteer	Money
Mueller	Volunteer	Adventure
Ott	Volunteer	Money
Perkins	Volunteer	Money/Blackmail
Thompson	Volunteer	Money/Disaffection
Wesson*	Volunteer	Money
Walton*	Volunteer	Money/Disaffection
Wood	Volunteer	Money/Adventure

* PSEUDONYMS

Recruitment and the Volunteer

Thompson (Chapter 5) provided three accounts of how he became involved in espionage. In the first, Thompson advised that in 1957, he had only 4 to 5 years remaining until he could retire, but his Commanding Officer was "giving him a hard time." Thompson started to drink heavily, was unfairly admonished for improper attire and appearance, and then his wife returned to the United States. He claims that he decided to seek asylum in East Germany and contacted the secret police;* however, they persuaded him to return and seek revenge by working for them as an espionage agent. In the second account, Thompson asserted that, in September 1955, he had become intimately involved with a woman and had been compromised by the secret police. Finally, Thompson claimed to be a Soviet "illegal" (see Chapter 5) dispatched by Soviet Intelligence to penetrate a U.S. Government agency or the military.

Investigators placed more credence on Thompson's first account, although there is some evidence to support his claim of being an illegal.[1]

In 1965, Thompson stated that he defected to East Germany because of personal problems, but upon returning to the West, he had regrets. Thompson maintains that he never kept the first meeting which had been scheduled, but that East German Intelligence Service (EGIS) officers picked him up on a street in West Berlin at gunpoint, forcing him to

---

*Thompson telephoned the East German Security Police with a number obtained from AFOSI counterintelligence files.

Volunteers

become a spy with threats and blackmail because of his "defection" to the East and intimate photographs of him with a woman.[2] Thompson is probably being truthful when he insists that the East Germans applied pressure on him concerning his defection (return to his unit and seek revenge), but the part about being picked up by gun-wielding East German Intelligence officers on a street in West Berlin seems farfetched[*] and more likely a rationalization, particularly in light of what he tells an interviewer from the Saturday Evening Post:

> I knew by now I was hooked. I was caught in the middle. So I told them all I knew. I cooperated with them. At first, it was out of fear. Later on that changed. They didn't have to use fear anymore. They warmed up to me and I warmed up to them. I cooperated with them 100% and I actually got so I worked hard at it.

DeChamplain (Chapter 5), an admitted homosexual, married a Thai woman in order to maintain a relationship with her brother, Sanan Juntsri, known as "Somchai." Somchai, a seaman in the Royal Thai Navy when he met DeChamplain, attempted to form a Thai "country and western" band after his discharge from the Navy and was supported by DeChamplain for 18 months. Shortly after their marriage, DeChamplain's wife, Nuan-Anung, moved out of their residence, but her

---

[*]Although there is no evidence to support Thompson's claim that he was kidnapped in West Berlin, such kidnappings did occur in the 1950's, but generally happened to Germans.

brother remained. At one time **DeChamplain** supported his wife, her two children from a previous marriage, her brother, and another dozen or so relatives and their friends all living in the same house. Although his wife moved out, he continued to send her money every month, as well as sending money to his parents in Connecticut.

DeChamplain claims that KGB officers were blackmailing him because of this homosexual relationship and that they also threatened to harm his mother and stepfather who lived in Connecticut. Neither of these assertions are believable. It would be extremely unlikely for the KGB to harm someone's parents residing in Connecticut and use heavy-handed blackmail threats over homosexuality. **DeChamplain** claims he told his KGB officer that he did not care if they exposed his homosexuality because he was eligible for retirement and would do so early if necessary to avoid the embarassment. Although blackmail frequently occurs in the Soviet Union and is conducted by the KGB's Second Chief Directorate (Internal Security), it is not a common practice for the KGB's First Chief Directorate (Foreign Intelligence), which primarily conducts operations in the West; however, within the Soviet Union, the FCD may employ this tactic.[3]

During this period in Bangkok, the Soviets were known to use local nationals acting as spotters, and, according to **DeChamplain**, he was introduced to a Soviet intelligence officer at a party in 1967, but this did not develop into a clandestine relationship until 1971 when his financial problems weakened his resolve and forced him to contact the

Volunteers

Soviets. **DeChamplain** was chronically in debt ($13,000 at the time of his arrest) and investigators have little doubt that he volunteered to work with the Soviets hoping to extricate himself from his financial difficulties. His statements concerning KGB blackmail and threats to his parents were nothing more than an attempt on his part to rationalize his betrayal of our country.[4]

Perkins (Chapter 5), after his arrest, said that he had been coerced and was only paid for his expenses. During interviews with counterintelligence officers, **Perkins** would not disclose how he had become involved with the Soviets, other than to say that he had been coerced. **Perkins** assertion that he was only "paid expenses," also was not accepted by investigators when it was learned that he had paid cash for a new Japanese car; made substantial investments in a bar in Japan in which he was part owner; and owned expensive furnishings and clothes. Additionally, after **Perkins'** arrest was reported by the media, it was learned that Soviet case officers had been instructed to advise their espionage agents that **Perkins** had been paid well for his espionage activities, contrary to press reports.[5]

In subsequent interviews, **Perkins** stated that he had walked in to the Soviet Embassy in Tokyo, in June or July 1966, and met with a GRU officer named Khavinov who remained his case officer. His claim that he walked in to the Soviet Embassy is most likely true; however, during the period he mentions, Khavinov was not assigned to the Soviet Embassy in

Tokyo. This discrepancy could have been the result of poor memory on **Perkins'** part or an intentional effort to mislead investigators.[6]

In subsequent interviews which occurred after his trial and conviction, **Perkins** advised that his motivation to commit espionage had resulted from blackmail by the Soviets. **Perkins** claimed that he had fathered an illegitimate child in 1966 while stationed in Vietnam and alleged to have sent money to the child and child's mother every month until September 1968, when the letters were returned. **Perkins** stated that he was approached by GRU officer Khavinov in December 1968, who told him that they were holding his child hostage and would harm the child unless **Perkins** cooperated.[7]

Perkins admitted that he provided some information, which was carefully selected so as not to cause serious damage to the USAF, and that when he returned to the United States in March 1969, such contacts ceased until May or June 1971. The situation then resurfaced, prompted by a GRU letter requesting him to attend a personal meeting in Mexico City.

Perkins' claim that he had walked in at the Soviet Embassy in Tokyo was essentially confirmed by polygraph examinations, whereas **Perkins'** assertion that the Soviets were holding his illegitimate child hostage could not be substantiated. It should also be noted that **Perkins** admitted that on several occasions he took the initiative to keep the contacts going or made suggestions to improve the security and method of operation.[8]

Volunteers

Kauffman (Chapter 5), who was traveling on leave in Germany, was arrested by East German police for riding on an unauthorized train. He claims the East Germans were pressuring him into becoming an espionage agent and allowed him to return to the West, with instructions to return the following day. Kauffman readily agreed and was quickly recruited and brought into a clandestine relationship.

Shortly thereafter, the EGIS case officer who recruited him defected, not only identifying Kauffman as an espionage agent and testifying at his trial, but also describing him as having been "easy" to recruit. Kauffman neither asked for nor received any money for the information he provided.[9] The motivating factors in this and all other cases will be discussed in detail in the following chapters.

According to a KGB training manual entitled, <u>The Practice of Recruiting Americans in the U.S. and Third Countries</u>,[10] the KGB lists the basic targets of agent penetration (operations) as follows:

- The President's Cabinet and the National Security Council;

- The State Department, including its representatives in New York, the U.S. delegation to the United States, the Passport Office of the State Department, and so forth;

- The U.S. Department of Defense (Pentagon), the military intelligence organs of this department, and the Permanent Military Group of the NATO Staff in the United States;

Recruitment and the Volunteer

- The Central Intelligence Agency and the Federal Bureau of Investigations;

- The National Association of Manufacturers, and the most important monopolies and banking houses, which have a direct influence on the U.S. Government;

- The most important scientific centers and laboratories; . . .

The KGB manual notes that Soviet intelligence officers must try to create or find conditions which ensure that the newly established contacts will not attract the attention of U.S. counterintelligence. The manual stresses that "the spotting, assessment, and selection of Americans for recruitment and the accomplishment of recruitment through recruiters remain the principal task of Soviet foreign intelligence in the U.S." The KGB and GRU systematically collect information on Americans who have intelligence potential in order to possibly make their acquaintance at a later date. The largest number of personnel with access to classified information are in the Department of Defense.

In a recent interview, ex-KGB Major Stanislav Levchenko was asked "Have you observed any personality patterns or background similarities in people willing to be spies?" Levchenko's response:[11]

> Lay people don't understand that, but professionals know that far more people are recruitable than one might think. All of us have weaknesses. We go through traumas in our lives, financial crises and all kinds of soul searching. Some people can handle them without losing their identity or determination and some people can't. I saw people recruited through all kinds of

17

vulnerabilities. Some people you might call ego maniacs were recruited because of that. Intelligence services exist because they know how vulnerabilities can be used. Picking the proper time and the proper people requires skill. Some people are vulnerable at one point in time, but a few months later are impossible to recruit. That's one reason why the KGB maintains such huge manpower in its foreign intelligence. You can screen 50 contacts to recruit one person. The degree of success can vary. Good intelligence officers must be good recruiters, or at least good gamblers. Recruiting is a very meticulous job, with a lot of research and a lot of psychology involved. It's difficult to describe someone perfectly suited for recruitment.

Vetting is generally the second phase of the recruitment process and involves the hostile intelligence service assessing the person who has been spotted as a potential spy to determine their suitability to commit espionage. Vetting occurs if the espionage agent is identified by the hostile intelligence service or the person volunteers to betray their country. Vetting is simply an indepth assessment of the potential agent's background, access to information, and motivation for betrayal. Foreign intelligence services will go to great lengths to gather information about their potential agents, attempting to confirm the information provided and most importantly, understanding the traitor's motivation. Telephone books, newspapers, reference books, and surveillance are used to gather applicable information.[12]

Recruitment and the Volunteer

Starting in the vetting phase and continuing until the formal recruitment, the foreign intelligence service may "cultivate" or socialize with the potential agent to determine his motives and weaknesses. One former GRU officer, who defected to the West, notes that the case officer may ask for small favors, gradually developing rapport and friendship with the agent who is being vetted until "one day the person will find all ways of extricating himself have been cut-off."[13]

Obviously, it is much easier for the hostile intelligence service to vet a volunteer because the volunteer has made the approach to become the spy and cooperates in providing the necessary background information needed to confirm and authenticate his or her identity, access, and motivation. However, this does not mean that volunteers are quickly deemed to be credible espionage agents. It may take even longer for the Soviets to believe in a volunteer than in someone they have found themselves. Whether a volunteer or not, traitors are never fully trusted.

Recruitment refers to the phase of the cycle when the hostile intelligence service has manipulated the potential spy into providing classified information. As discussed earlier, many individuals who have been "recruited" were actually volunteers. Regardless of how the person is spotted and vetted, if a relationship develops to the stage of recruitment, the potential agent has very likely been sending out positive signals concerning his or her susceptibility to become involved in espionage. **DeChamplain** is a typical case example of this phenomenon.

Volunteers

It is important to note that the word "recruitment" implies a positive action to spot, vet, and recruit a spy, but recruitment is a misnomer when discussing espionage in the Air Force. The overwhelming majority of USAF traitors (21 cases) made the spotting, vetting, and recruitment process easier by bringing themselves to the attention of the hostile intelligence service.

Throughout the spotting and vetting phases, the hostile intelligence officer is searching for the "key" which will unlock the potential agent's motivation to respond favorably to the recruitment pitch. The case officer invests considerable time in attempting to determine motivation, regardless of whether the agent is a volunteer or is sought out by the hostile intelligence service. One former KGB defector describes the recruitment process with the acronym MICE, which stands for Money, Ideology, Compromise, and Ego. One or more of these characteristics can be used to motivate a person to become involved in espionage or to continue to be involved, once that fateful involvement has begun.[14]

During World War II, the Abwehr* also relied on three factors (other than youth, willingness, or threat of death to serve) when considering motivation, and, prioritized, these are:[15]

- Lure of easy money

- Danger

- Idealism

---

*One of several German intelligence and counterintelligence oganizations operating throughout World War II.

Recruitment and the Volunteer

A cursory examination of USAF espionage cases reveals that lucre is by far the most frequent motivational factor, although after arrest many traitors attempted to explain and rationalize their reason for betrayal to be something less dishonorable than the desire for money. In many cases, danger and excitement are also strong contributing factors.

Whereas the KGB tends to be more cautious and formal in their recruitment pitch, the GRU case officer appears to be less cautious and often does not undertake a formal recruitment pitch. The agent is considered recruited when he provides information and accepts payment.[16]

According to Viktor Suvorov, a former GRU officer, the GRU relies on two principal methods of recruitment. The first is a gradual process, which requires many personal meetings to assess the potential spy, and is extremely risky. The second is referred to as the "crash approach" and involves the case officer recruiting the agent as quickly as possible to avoid risky meetings.[17]

Although this crash or blunt approach (also known as a "cold approach") is often used, it probably is not very successful, but could be used when the case officer is under pressure to quickly recruit an agent or is faced with some other type of urgent situation. It may also be a favored approach for the less confident case officer or intelligence service (particularly in totalitarian countries). The cold approach would be more successful because the security apparatus can exert more control and fear over the targeted individual.

Volunteers

Regardless of how recruitment is made, intelligence doctrine emphasizes the need to strengthen and reinforce the motivation of the agent as soon as possible to establish and maintain control. For example, it is not unusual to have the agent told that he or she has been promoted or awarded a medal (**Walker**); sign a receipt for equipment (**Thompson**) or money (**Wesson**) received; or receive promises of additional money (**DeChamplain**).

During its early stages, the recruitment process occurs through face-to-face (personal) meetings which are usually held in restaurants, cafes, cars, or public parks. Safehouses are not commonly used at this stage of the clandestine relationship. The recruitment phase is one of the most dangerous periods of the relationship for both the hostile intelligence service case officer and the potential traitor because a safe and clandestine means of communication has yet to be established.[18]

Once an agent has been recruited or volunteers, it is normal practice to improve the security of the operation by establishing clandestine communication channels. Some Air Force traitors, who have become involved in espionage, received little or no training in the principles of tradecraft (**Ahadi** and **Kauffman**), whereas others (**Perkins**, **Boeckenhaupt**, and **Bronson**) received considerable training.

One of the most notable instances of such training is the **Thompson** case. He not only received extensive tradecraft training and equipment, but the majority of the instruction was conducted in the Soviet Union.

Recruitment and the Volunteer

    The most common forms of clandestine agent communication are secret writing and dead drops. These and other methods of communication will be discussed in the following chapter.

Chapter 3

CLANDESTINE COMMUNICATIONS

For spies to be successful at espionage, they must obtain information and communicate it to the hostile intelligence service for which they work. A wide variety of methods exist to communicate with spymasters, but the spy needs some means of protecting the information and any clandestine communication equipment that is issued.[1] Concealment devices are employed to hide a spy's espionage tradecraft items, his or her means of production, or both. Although concealment devices and clandestine communication equipment are not always issued to spies (and when issued, they are difficult for counterintelligence investigators to detect), their discovery could lead to valuable evidence--the method and means a suspect uses to communicate with the hostile intelligence service involved.

Concealment is employed when it is necessary to hide the existence of a person, place, or thing. The purpose of a concealment device is to disguise or hide an object of operational significance, so that it appears to be something else, having no relationship to the clandestine operation.

Practically anything can be used or modified for use as a concealment device, depending on the size and shape of the object to be concealed. A simple package wrapped as a gift or a highly sophisticated modification of a coin, such as the hollowed nickel discovered in the investigation of Rudolf Abel, may serve as a concealment device.[2] The primary requirement for the hostile intelligence service to consider in providing a concealment device to an espionage agent is the operational need for the device to maintain the security of the clandestine relationship.

Occasionally, concealment devices are constructed with built-in security traps that may detonate or destroy the material hidden if an attempt is made by an uninformed person to open the device. Often devices are designed only for one-time use and must be broken open in order to obtain the hidden material.[3] **Bronson** (Chapter 5) was provided a fake rock by his GRU case officer which was to be used to conceal material at a dead drop location in Bedfordshire, England.[4] **Thompson** (Chapter 5) was given a special pair of shoes and a tiny screwdriver, three-quarters of an inch long. The screwdriver was used to slip into a tiny nail hole in the back of the heels on each shoe. A locking mechanism was released and the heel came off. One heel had been hollowed out in order to conceal two rolls of Minox film and the other heel had been hollowed out in order to conceal "suicide" capsules which **Thompson** claimed his KGB case officer had given him to use if he was arrested.[5] **Thompson** was also provided a cigarette case concealing a one-time-pad (OTP) which was used to decode radio messages sent from the Soviet Union.[6]

In many espionage operations, communications pose the most difficult problem for the hostile intelligence services and their spies. It is often comparatively simple to obtain wanted information, perhaps by bribery or coercion, or even by overt observation. The difficulties arise when the

Volunteers

information has to be conveyed to those who want it before it becomes outdated and therefore of no value. Many spies have been caught attempting to overcome this problem, and hostile intelligence services go to great lengths to devise ways to communicate safely. The only perfectly secure way for a foreign intelligence service to operate is to have no personal or impersonal contact between the handler and his agent. But as logic dictates, communication between the case officer and his agent must occur. Communication is the weakest link in any clandestine relationship and thus susceptible to detection by counterintelligence investigators.

For the espionage efforts of a hostile intelligence service to be successful, a clandestine means of communication must be established between the hostile intelligence case officer (HCO) and the espionage agent. There are two general categories of clandestine communications, personal and impersonal.[7] The first of these, personal, is the most dangerous, as it involves a face-to-face meeting between the hostile intelligence officer and his agent. The physical presence of the HCO and his agent together automatically links them in some type of relationship if they are observed.

Personal meetings are not held without a specific operational reason. The personal meeting allows the case officer to make on-the-spot decisions concerning his agent. He may be able to iron out any problems, boost morale, detect changes in the agent's attitude, motivation, and personality; provide training; and assess the agent's capabilities.

A meeting between a case officer and his agent is the most vulnerable form of communication. In organizing a meeting, the case officer must anticipate the unexpected if security of the operation is to be maintained. Obviously, the meeting time and place are important; however, the case officer must also have a detailed and specific agenda and a cover story in the event they are observed. The first item covered at a personal meeting is to make arrangements for future meetings in case the meeting is interrupted. New agents or those under development must be met more frequently.

Of the two types of clandestine communication, the second method, impersonal, is by far the safer. Impersonal communication includes all other methods of communications which do not place the case officer and his agent in direct personal contact. Impersonal communication methods separate the intelligence case officer and his agent by either time, space, or location. During the spotting, assessing, and recruitment phase, the HCO initially will rely on personal meetings with the potential agent; however, once they are recruited and as they gain experience, impersonal means of communication will be established to protect the security of the operation.[8] Impersonal means of communication offers a variety of advantages. First, this method of communication provides for maximum operational security. Next, it is more flexible to use than to arrange a personal meeting. Finally, the hostile intelligence services can initiate and control when and how the communication is to occur. It should be noted that two disadvantages of impersonal communication also exist. First, it is difficult to conduct discussions or very thorough briefings and debriefings. Second, the communication could be accidentally or intentionally intercepted.

Once the operation has transited to the action phase, the case officer will employ a variety of impersonal clandestine communication methods to communicate safely and to exchange information and material with their agents.

A dead drop (DD) is a location which has been selected because it can provide an avenue for the HCO and his agent to exchange information and thus communicate, yet it reduces the inherent risks involved with personal meetings. The dead drop site in Maryland used by GRU Colonel Izmaylov* to obtain classified information from an Air Force officer is typical of sites often selected by the GRU, KGB, and other intelligence services.

Obviously, if personal meetings are dangerous and the traitor has a considerable number of documents to provide, a dead drop is an ideal method for safely exchanging information. Traitors will load DD with classified information; HCO will load DD with money, instructions, and espionage tradecraft materials (Figure 5).

In the United States, the Soviets frequently use rural areas, but the HCO and the traitor must have logical reasons

---

*GRU Colonel Izmaylov, assigned to the Soviet Military Mission in Washington, DC, as the Air Attache, was detained unloading a DD containing classified material. The material had been placed there by a USAF officer working under the control and direction of AFOSI and FBI counterintelligence officers.

for being in the area, in the event they are observed. Historically, the Soviets have used parks, fields, wooded areas, and small country lanes for their dead drop locations in conducting espionage against the Air Force.[9]

The HCO and his agent must be able to find the exact location of the dead drop. In some cases (John Walker), the Soviets will provide maps, photographs, even drawing routes and instructions.[10] The GRU provided photographs of the selected dead drop sites, as well as maps to **Bronson**, so that he could easily find the right location to be used.[11] According to one GRU defector,[12] the GRU will only use a dead drop location just once. In actual practice, it is not unusual for the GRU or KGB to use a dead drop location more than once. As a general rule, it could be assumed that the GRU does not want an agent to use the same dead drop location repeatedly; however, residencies, case offices, or both, may deviate for various reasons, such as mistakes, laziness, or operational concerns.

In conjunction with the dead drop location, intelligence services employ signals to alert the case officer, the agent, or both, that the dead drop has been loaded or unloaded. Signals, usually visual, may consist of stamps, chalk marks, masking tape, crushed cigarette packs, or cans left in a specific place at a specific time. **James Wood** left red chalk marks under a designated park bench in San Francisco, whereas John Walker left a soft drink can alongside a Maryland road which was designated by the KGB. GRU Colonel Izmaylov instructed his agent to use a soft drink can on one occasion and another time to use a Christmas tree ornament left alongside a country lane. The location where the signal is made is known as a signal site.

Signal sites are not located near the drop or meeting sites. The signals used would have meanings which were previously agreed upon and known only to the intelligence service and the traitor. For example, to signal for a meeting in East Berlin, Thompson was instructed by the KGB to check for a roofing nail stuck in a certain wooden telephone pole on the Obentrautstrame. The meeting would then be held the next night at a time and location which were previously agreed upon.[13]

Basically, the person placing material at the dead drop (normally dead drop refers to location; the material being exchanged is usually left in some type of container or concealment device) will load the drop, and then make a signal at the agreed-upon location and time. The person unloading the drop will check the first signal, proceed to the drop, and retrieve the material being exchanged and then make a signal at another prearranged location and time, which will be checked by the person who loaded the drop. The signals not only help to easily determine if a drop has been loaded or unloaded, but also act as a safety device. If there is no signal, then the agent or the case officer will not approach the dead drop site.

The Soviets use dead drops to provide instructions, money, clandestine communication equipment, or any other item necessary to maintain the operation. The agent in turn will load the dead drop with his production (intelligence information, documents, photographs, sketches, and so forth). Even though modern technology has created sophisticated electronic opportunities of clandestine communication between the Soviets and their agents, dead drops are still required in most fully developed espionage operations. First, the Soviets have no desire to provide sophisticated electronic equipment to every agent they handle because the agent could be arrested or may be operating under the control of Western counterintelligence. Second, sophisticated electronic communication devices can only be used in conjunction with a communications plan and the plan must be provided through a personal meeting (which is highly dangerous) or some other method. Finally, in countries where the Soviets believe their signals may be intercepted, dead drops remain the most reliable method to communicate safely with their agents.

Even with sophisticated satellite communications, the tried-and-true method of using dead drops probably will never be eliminated. The Soviets are not going to give every agent a sophisticated, expensive, and sensitive piece of equipment, and, in most cases, it would be unnecessary. In general, they will communicate with their agents as they have always done and only provide sensitive electronic communication devices to their most valuable agents, when required by operational necessity.

An accommodation address (AA) is an address provided by the hostile intelligence service to their agent where posted mail is received, held for pickup, or transmitted to a person

Volunteers

who does not regularly occupy the premises. The individual operating the AA may be witting or unwitting and will not open any mail posted to him. The outside of the envelope or the postcard will be marked in some previously agreed-upon way to indicate that the mail is related to the hostile intelligence services clandestine operations. When mailing a letter or postcard to an accommodation address, the spy is normally instructed to use a false name. Letters containing secret writing that are sent to the AA are usually forwarded to the residency* where they may be opened.

In some cases, Moscow Headquarters will identify letters to the residency which are not to be opened at the residency. These letters are usually from extremely valuable agents being run directly from Moscow. Generally speaking, AA's are not used by an agent to send his production (intelligence information) to the hostile service, but are used to arrange or cancel meetings, request instructions or money, and to reestablish contact when arriving in a new country of assignment.

One of the best examples of how a hostile intelligence service may utilize an AA is found in the case of Boeckenhaupt (Chapter 5). The GRU provided him with AA's in Bangkok, Thailand, and London, England to be used upon his return to the United States after finishing his assignment in

---

*The "residency" is the office or work area from which the KGB and GRU directs intelligence activities. Usually, the residency is located within the Soviet Embassy, but it may be located within any other Soviet establishment as well.

Morocco.[14] To reestablish contact with the GRU in the United States, Boeckenhaupt was instructed to mail a letter (using secret writing (SW) in an innocent-sounding letter) in October 1963 to an AA in Bangkok to arrange for a meeting in December 1963. The meeting was held in Alexandria, Virginia, and was used by the Soviets to establish Boeckenhaupt's identity and provide him with new instructions. Boeckenhaupt also used SW in letters mailed to the London address to arrange meetings in Washington, DC with his case officer in November 1965 and April 1966.[15]

After being reassigned from Texas to California, Boeckenhaupt claimed he could find little information of value to the Soviets and that it was difficult for him to travel to Washington, DC for personal meetings. In August 1966, Boeckenhaupt's need for money forced him to send another letter to the London AA asking the Soviets to meet him in California and provide money. After receiving no response, he sent a second letter.

Shortly thereafter (Boeckenhaupt surmised that his second letter crossed in the mail with the Soviets response to his first letter) he received a response from the Soviets to his request for a meeting and believed the Soviets were attempting to arrange a meeting with him in California. Although Boeckenhaupt believes the Soviets would have met him in California, there is no evidence to support his belief other than his opinion. It would have been highly unusual (as well as risky) for the Soviets to have met with

Volunteers

Boeckenhaupt, unless they felt that his value as an agent warranted such a drastic step. Boeckenhaupt was arrested before the proposed meeting occurred.[16]

From the beginnings of Soviet rule following the October 1917 Revolution, the Soviet expansion into foreign countries raised technical problems regarding timely clandestine communications. Although early Soviet codes and ciphers were weak and extensively read by the unauthorized, the concept of communication security was quickly developed. Felixs Dzhershinsky, the first Chairman of the Cheka[*] (the forerunner of today's KGB) demanded that all communications be enciphered and handled as if they were highly incriminating. Messages were to be cryptically written, as well as concealed within the writing. Today, secret writing is still used extensively by the Soviet intelligence services to communicate with their espionage agents. SW is used to conceal written operational information and is used in regular mail channels in conjunction with an accommodation address.

In general, there are three types of secret writing systems: wet, transfer, and microphotographic.[17] Wet secret writing systems use colorless fluids as "inks" (however, a true "ink" is not "colorless"). These inks range from basic to sophisticated. Wet systems consist of two types: organic and sympathetic chemicals.[18] Examples of organic substances are milk, blood, urine, and citrus

---

*Chrevzuychaynaya Komissiya Po Borbe s Kontrarevolutsiyei i Sabotazhen or Extraordinary Commission to Combat Counterrevolution, Speculation and Sabotage. The Cheka's symbol was a serpent with a sword hanging over its head.

juice, and these are developed when exposed to heat. Sympathetic chemical substances are soluble chemicals which are developed when exposed to chemical vapors or solutions. Modern day SW may use highly sophisticated inks composed of specific chemicals in precise quantities which may only be developed with a specific formula. To ensure that the SW will work, it is not unusual to find the chemicals made into capsules, pills, or liquids.[19] Chemical inks are invisible when dry, but become visible when the paper they are used on is treated with a specific reagent.[20]

Transfer SW systems are more commonly known as "carbons."[21] SW carbons are the most common type of SW system found, primarily because they are more easily employed. The carbons are nothing more than paper which has been specially treated with chemicals. These paper sheets (which will appear to be ordinary paper) are used like tracing paper and placed over a letter or paper which contains an innocent message. When writing between the lines of the innocent letter and pressing down on the chemically impregnated paper, the invisible chemical is deposited onto the letter. It is then mailed to an accommodation address and forwarded to a residency or the Soviet Union, where a special developer is used to retrieve the SW.

The carbons are easy to conceal because they appear to be ordinary paper and agents are usually instructed to keep them with a similar type of paper. To easily distinguish the SW carbon from ordinary paper, the Soviets often will have the carbons as the last two or three pages of the book or pad of

Volunteers

paper. Thompson was given an American-made address book and the SW carbons were inserted as the last two pages, but they appeared to be like any other page in the book. He was instructed to use each page several times before destroying them.[22]

The Thompson case provides a typical example of how the Soviets use secret writing with an espionage agent. Before his reassignment from Germany to the United States, the Soviets brought Thompson to the Soviet Union for tradecraft training. He was instructed to write on a hard surface such as a desk top made of glass. His female training officer told him to lay out a sheet of writing paper lengthwise--not up and down--and then place the SW carbon on top. Thompson was instructed to put another sheet on top of the carbon and write with a stylus or dry ballpoint pen in clear block letters. He was told to destroy the top sheet of paper and to save the SW carbon in the back of his address book to be used again. Thompson would then turn the paper around--top to bottom--and write an innocent letter.[23]

The final category of secret writing which has been used by hostile intelligence services in directing espionage agents against the Air Force is microphotography. A microdot is an optically (photographed) reduced negative (image), using aniline-based photosensitive particles, which results in a page of text being reduced to the size of a period on a standard typewriter.[24]

Historically, microdots have been used for intelligence purposes since the siege of Paris in 1870 when France was at war with Prussia. The size of microdots at that time was 70mm and contained 300,000 characters; microdots were sent via balloons and pigeons.[25]

Because the preparation of microdots requires special photographic equipment which would be suspect, unless the spy had appropriate cover as a professional photographer or had an established hobby of photography, microphotography is usually confined to headquarters-to-agent communication.[26]

The Nazis have been given credit for inventing microdots;[27] however, Commander Foote, a British and Soviet agent, notes in his book, <u>Handbook for Spies</u>, that the Soviet intelligence services had been using microdots before World War II. Although the German Nazis did not invent microdots, there is considerable evidence that they made important contributions to the development of microdot technology and used microdots aggressively throughout the world prior to and during World War II to run espionage agents. One model (a 6-foot-long optical bench) used by the Nazis' to produce microdots, weighed 4,200 pounds and used handmade spread emulsion on glass sheets; it was supplied from Berlin by the Abwehr to officers assigned to field units. Another model fit into a satchel and used high-resolution emulsion and thin film backing.[28]

The British also used microdots during the war and accomplished their task by using 35mm negatives as an intermediate layer, which was then backed away from a negative 50 inches, with each camera having to be individually calibrated. It is believed that the British used high-resolution spectrographic film coated on glass slides in their process.[29]

Microphotography may also include the use of positive-type film, as opposed to negative-type film, and a bleaching of the image prior to dispatch occurs so that it appears as a clear piece of cellophane or thin plastic. This product of microphotography is referred to as a "mikrat" which was extensively developed by the Germans during World War II.[30] Today, mikrats measure 1mm by 1mm and are the most commonly employed form of microdot used by the Soviets.

The Soviets will often use thin plastic or cellophane to provide instructions to their agents (Figure 4). Although a chemical process similar to making microdots and mikrats is used, these thin plastic sheets or cellophanes are not reduced to the same size as microdots or mikrats and can often be easily read, once developed, without any special microscope or equipment.

Thompson was trained by the KGB in the use of microphotography on a trip to the Soviet Union. He was instructed to use a 35mm reflex camera and to lay the document he was photographing on a flat table. He would then clamp the camera to a chair (or anything which could hold the camera steady) and take the picture. After its development, he would place the negative between two glass slides to hold it flat and then take a piece of ordinary cellophane and make it light sensitive with specially prepared chemicals provided by the Soviets. He would then put a piece of white paper on the flat surface, clamping a small microdot camera over the paper.

Thompson described the microdot camera as being a small brass tube, about 1-1/2 inches long with lenses at both ends. Exactly 35 inches above the bottom end of the microdot camera he would clamp a glass plate with the negative and above that a 3 by 1 power hand magnifying glass. Over the magnifying glass, he placed a 100-watt, clear-glass electric light, causing the light to shine through the magnifying glass and then the negative and microdot camera. **Thompson** had to raise and lower the glass until he could clearly focus the negative on the tiniest possible spot on the piece of white paper on the flat table. He then marked the spot with an X, turned off the light, and, after about 3 minutes, took the cellophane out and developed it with regular commercial developer. After the cellophane was developed, he could see a little black dot on the cellophane about the size of a period. He broke off a corner of a razor blade and, using the sharp pointed edge, cut out the spot (microdot).

Taking a postcard, **Thompson** made a 1/16-inch deep slit in one edge and picked up the microdot with tweezers, slipped it into the slot, and sealed the slot with paste made from flour and water "because other pastes contain bone marrow and that would show up under ultraviolet light." **Thompson** kept his microdot camera hidden in a regular standard-size flashlight dry-cell battery, which actually worked.[31]

As can be seen from **Thompson's** description, preparing microdots is a difficult and time-consuming process. Additionally, once the microdot is mailed, there is always the risk that it will fall off or out of the postcard or letter; that the case officer receiving the letter will be

Volunteers

unable to locate the concealed microdot; or that the case officer will accidentally lose it once it is located. The training and skill required of the espionage agent, coupled with the problems associated with accidental losses, explains why microphotography is not frequently used. The speed and simplicity of the SW carbon makes this the most efficient SW system to communicate within a clandestine manner.

Radio communication frequently encountered in clandestine communication, commonly referred to as One-Way-Voice-Link (OWVL), is used for headquarters to agent communication. The headquarters, operating in controlled (friendly) areas, is not concerned with discovery through monitoring and direction finding. Broadcasts are usually on short-wave frequencies and the transmission will be coded or encrypted and on a prearranged schedule. The espionage agent will reply through another means of clandestine communication.[32] Suvorov notes that the Soviets will broadcast from radio stations, ships, and polar stations; and this broadcast can be received on ordinary radio receivers.[33]

Thompson received OWVL broadcasts from the Soviets after he was reassigned from Germany to the United States. He was instructed to learn the German phrase "Die Buchandlungen Wirtschaf" and then write it on paper in the shape of the letter T with "Die Buchandlungen" on top and "Wirtschaf" underneath on the shaft of the T. The letters were then numbered starting at the bottom of the shaft and then across the top from left to right. This phrase was used in conjunction with a cipher code pad, more commonly referred to as a one-time-pad (OTP) because each page is used only once.

The OTP had 20 sheets and each sheet had columns of five-digit numbers. **Thompson** listened to shortwave radio every Thursday morning at 0705 until he heard his signal "Amur Ya Lena." The message came in numbers, five digits at a time, spoken in Russian. It told him which sheet of the OTP to use and to subtract the numbers on the OTP from those received in the radio message. After subtracting, he was to count on the letter T until he came to that number and it would be the letter he needed to construct a word. Each five-digit group of numbers equated to one letter.[34]

The primary purpose of clandestine communication (other than security) is to transmit information between the espionage agent and his handling officer. Although verbal information and actual documents may be obtained and passed to a hostile intelligence service, frequently this is impossible. Photography is thus extensively employed by the agent to photograph those documents which either cannot be removed or may be too bulky to be stored and transmitted in any fashion. Basically two types of espionage cameras exist--one is specially made by the hostile intelligence service (commonly referred to as a "rollover" camera by Western counterintelligence, however, it is called a "brush" camera by the Soviets), but the other may be commercially purchased.

Rollover cameras, similar to the one illustrated in Figures 2 and 3, are specially made cameras designed only for the purpose of taking photographs of documents. The camera has two small rubber wheels and when these are rolled across

Volunteers

a page of a document, will activate the photographic mechanism, to include a built-in light source. It takes three passes with the camera on each page in order to photograph the entire page. Approximately 40 pages can be photographed in this manner before the film cassette must be replaced. Commercial cameras are more frequently encountered.[35]

Thompson was given a commercially available H-Minox 35mm camera, after receiving 1-1/2 hours of training, and was required to sign for it.[36] The KGB was preparing to provide training and a Minox camera to **DeChamplain**; however, he was arrested by AFOSI before the training could be accomplished.[37] **Bronson** was given a Minox camera by the GRU (which he subsequently pawned because he needed the money) and 20 rolls of film.[38] **Mira** (Chapter 5) used his own personal 35mm camera to take photographs of documents in his duty section at night[39] and **Boeckenhaupt** used a Minox camera to take photographs of classified documents for the GRU.[40]

To improve its operation, a commercially acquired camera may be modified by the foreign intelligence service or they may provide the agent with specially prepared lenses, adapters, and film. Film provided will be disguised as a brand frequently purchased by the average photographer; however, the film is protected and requires special developers to expose it.

Clandestine Communications

Clandestine communication to transfer information and material is considered to be the weakest link between the hostile intelligence service and the traitor. Although sophisticated methods of communication have been employed in the past, the foreign intelligence service is only required to provide the agent with the minimum amount of training and equipment to ensure that the clandestine relationship remains undetected and the agent is able to transmit the information to the case officer. In some successful espionage operations, the traitor was given very little training or equipment, yet managed to cause considerable damage to our national security.

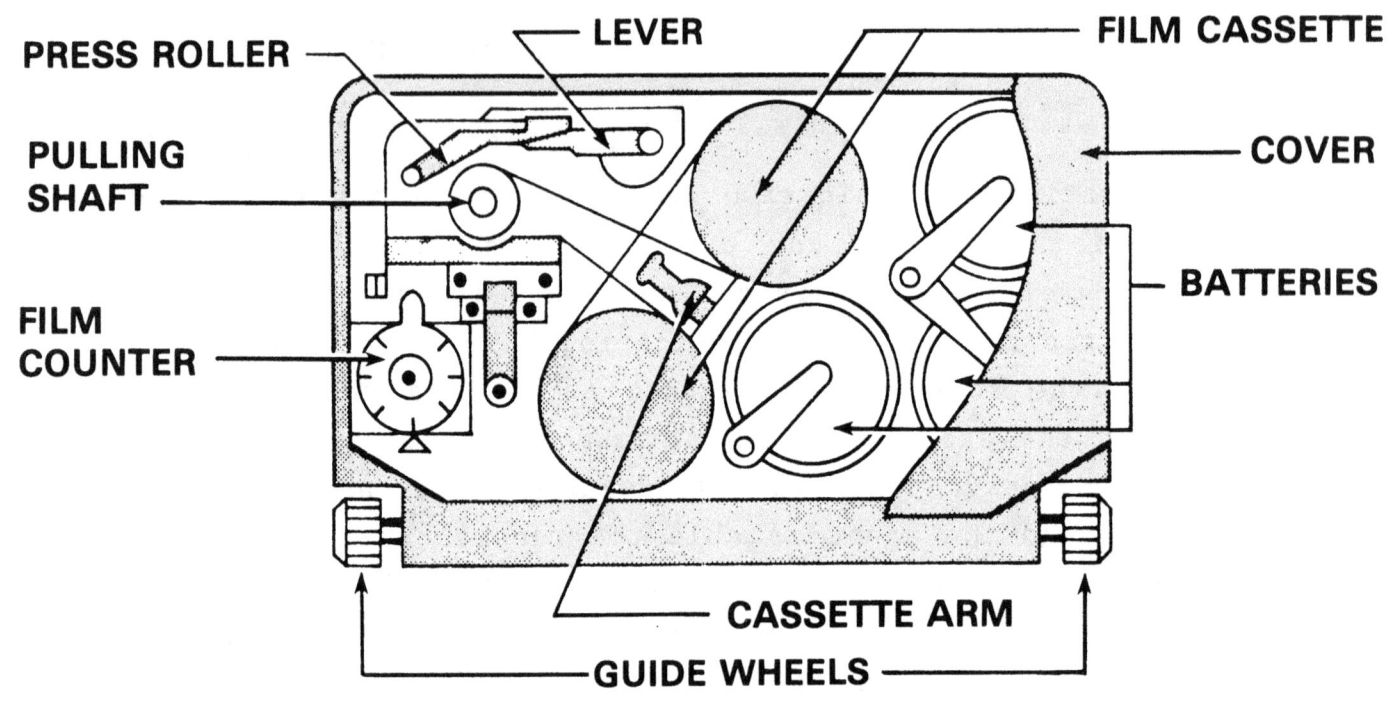
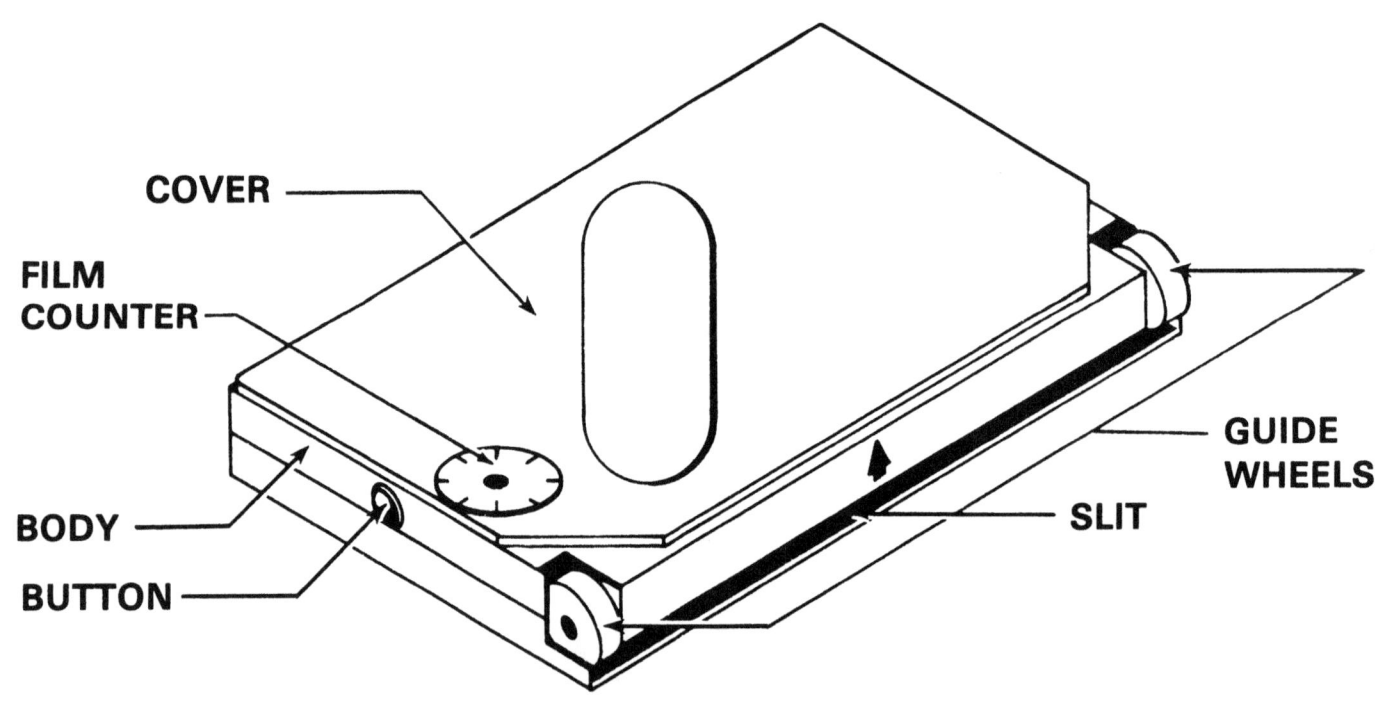

ROLLOVER CAMERA

44

Clandestine Communications

Figure 3

This rollover camera (depicted with outside cover removed) was provided to an Air Force officer by GRU Colonel Vladimir Izmaylov to photograph classified documents pertaining to Stealth and Strategic Defense Initiative technology. The camera is designed to photograph documents inside secure work areas and can only be used to photograph documents. It is estimated that it costs $25,000 for a rollover camera to be constructed. At the top left-and right-hand corners of the camera are rubber rollers which are placed on the document page to be photographed and then rolled across the page activating the photographic mechanism. It requires three passes across one page if the espionage agent is to photograph the entire page. Power is provided by three silver-colored batteries and the film cassette contains enough film to photograph 40 pages. Adjacent to the film cassette can be seen instructions for the agent on how to properly load the film into the camera. (AFOSI Investigative Case File)

Volunteers

Figure 4

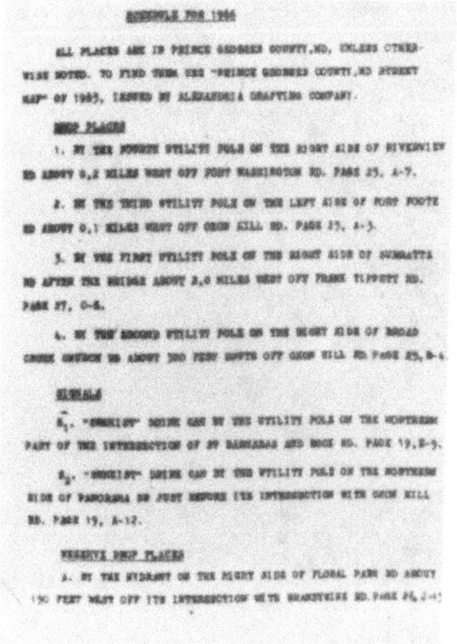

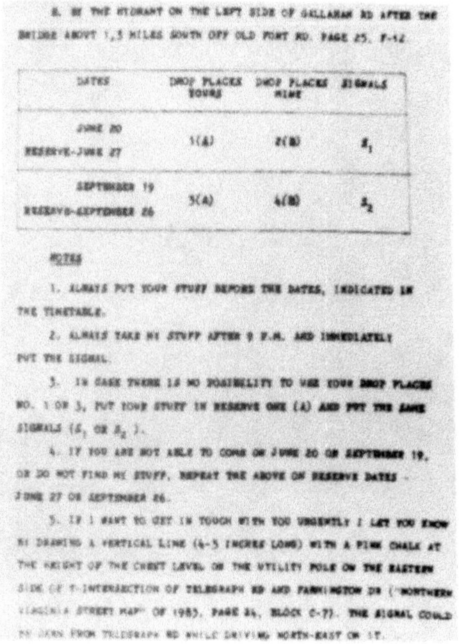

Photograph of cellophane enlarged to show the clandestine meet instructions provided by GRU Colonel Izmaylov to an Air Force officer working under the control and direction of AFOSI. The cellophane is very thin film and feels similar to the wrapping around cigarette packages. The information contained on the cellophane is latent (invisible) and requires special chemical developers to bring out the image. The cellophane describes the dead drop, signals, and reserve drop locations to be used to communicate clandestinely with the GRU in 1986. Directions are provided, as well as special instructions on how to load and unload the dead drops and what to do if a dead drop cannot be loaded as specified on the schedule. (AFOSI Investigative Case File)

Clandestine Communications

Figure 5

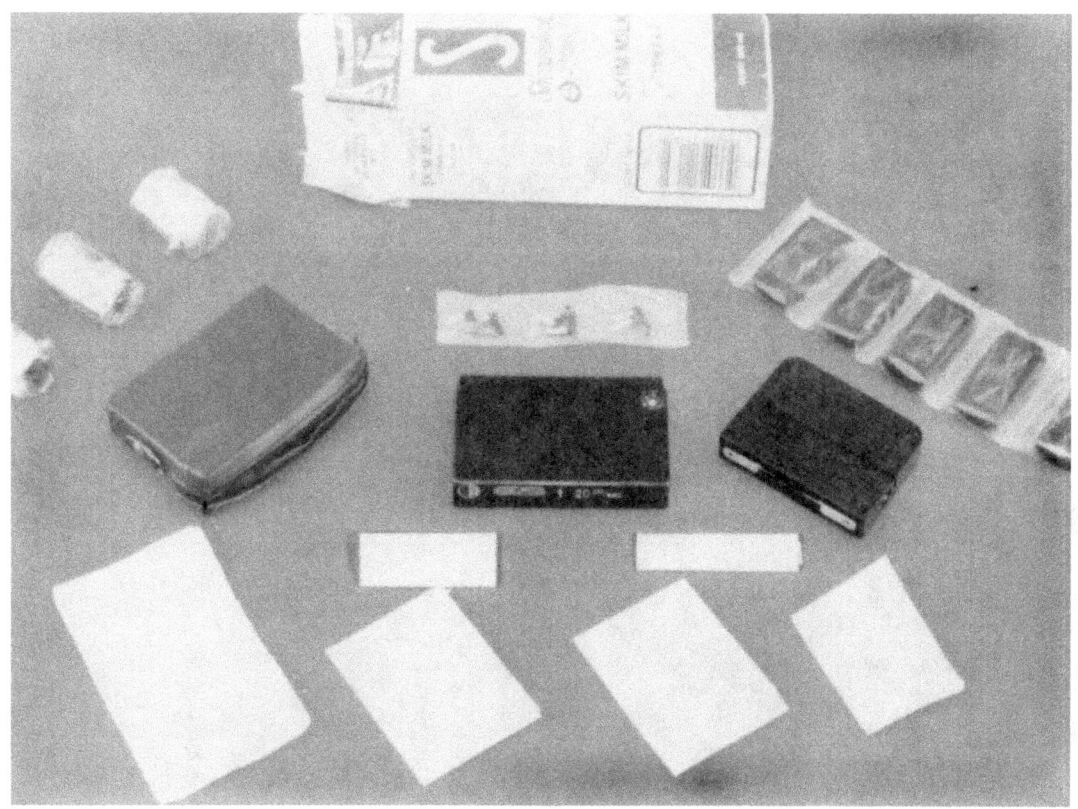

This photograph illustrates items provided by the GRU to an Air Force officer at a dead drop in a rural area near Washington, DC. The GRU used a milk carton to hold the material being provided to the espionage agent. In the milk carton was a rollover camera, a leather case for the camera, a battery charger to charge the camera batteries, five film cassettes each containing 120 exposures, spare light bulbs for the camera, and instructions on how to operate the camera. Additionally, the milk carton contained $15,000 in cash (the three rolls on the left of the photograph) and a map with instructions for future dead drops. (AFOSI Investigative Case File)

Volunteers

(LEFT-Figure 6) Herbert Boeckenhaupt after his arrest for committing treason on behalf of the GRU. (AFOSI Investigative Case File)

(RIGHT-Figure 7) Ray DeChamplain was arrested in Bangkok, Thailand, after several contacts with KGB officers. When arrested he was attempting to provide the KGB with a Top Secret document. (AFOSI Investigative Case File)

Illustration

Figure 8

2Lt Christopher M. Cooke, pictured here in the custody of Air Force Security Police, visited the Soviet Embassy in Washington, DC, in 1980, and did not report his visits as required by Air Force Regulations. (AFOSI Investigative Case File)

Volunteers

Figure 9

SSgt **Guiseppe Cascio**, along with **John Jones**, attempted to sell classified information to North Korea in 1953. (Wide World Photo Service)

Illustration

Figure 10

A1C Gustav Mueller, a 19-year-old student at an intelligence school in Germany was arrested in 1949 after attempting to sell classified information to Soviet Intelligence officers, who, in reality, were counterintelligence officers. (Wide World Photo Service)

Figure 11

Capt French and his wife Dorothy in a photograph taken several years before his arrest for espionage. He was a highly decorated World War II and Korean War combat navigator and bombardier. (AFOSI Investigative Case File)

Illustration

(LEFT-Figure 12) **Capt French**, as he appeared early in his Air Force career, was arrested after throwing a note on the grounds of the Soviet Military Mission. U.S. counterintelligence officers, posing as Soviet intelligence officers, arrested him in his hotel room in New York City. French led investigators to a locker which contained classified documents that he was hoping to sell to the Soviet Union in order to pay off gambling debts exceeding $8,000. (AFOSI Investigative Case File)

(RIGHT-Figure 13) **Capt Kauffman** was arrested on a train in East Germany and volunteered to commit treason for the East German Intelligence Service. (AFOSI Investigative Case file)

Volunteers

(LEFT-Figure 14)**Airman Ott**, an administrative clerk, contacted the Soviet Consulate in San Francisco and offered to sell classified information concerning the SR-71 aircraft. Ott was arrested and sentenced to 25 years in prison. (AFOSI Investigative Case File)

(RIGHT-Figure 15)**Walter Perkins** who was arrested boarding a plane to Mexico City in 1971 to meet his GRU case officer. In his possession was a briefcase containing over 600 pages of classified information. Perkins claimed to have been blackmailed by the Soviets, however, there is little evidence to support his story. (AFOSI Investigative Case File)

Illustration

(LEFT-Figure 16) **TSgt James Wood**, several months prior to his arrest. He had been granted a waiver from Air Force dress and appearance regulations because of his investigative duties. Wood considered himself to be a "flashy" dresser and a "ladies' man." (RIGHT-Figure 17) Wood in a photograph taken shortly after his arrest in New York City. A garbage bag was found in his nearby rental car which contained almost 200 classified documents that Wood would have provided to the KGB if he had not been arrested by the FBI. (AFOSI Investigative Case File)

Volunteers

(LEFT-Figure 18) **Robert Thompson** pictured after his arrest for providing classified information to the KGB. He was extensively trained by the KGB in the Soviet Union on secret writing, microphotography, and one-way-voice-link (radio) procedures to enable him to remain in contact with his case officers. **Thompson** was believed to have provided support to KGB "illegals" who were provided false identity documents and backgrounds so that they could covertly enter the United States. (RIGHT-Figure 19) This photograph of **Thompson** was taken shortly before he was exchanged to East Germany in 1978 for an Israeli pilot being held in Mozambique. His return to the Eastern Bloc was unusual and lends some credence to his claim that he was a Soviet "illegal" who had entered the United States under fabricated documents and assumed a false identity in order to infiltrate the Air Force. (AFOSI Investigative Case File)

Illustration

Figure 20

KGB officer Alex Malinin who was handling **Herbert Boeckenhaupt** in Washington, DC after **Boeckenhaupt** established contact in Morocco. (Wide World Photo Service)

Volunteers

 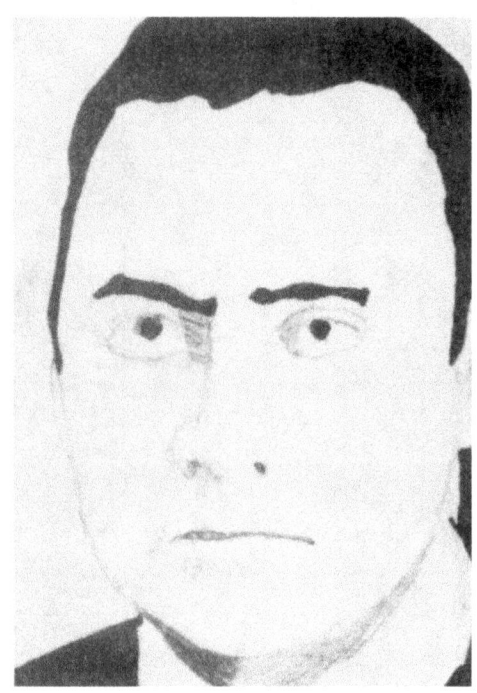

(LEFT-Figure 21) East German Intelligence Service officer Lt Guneter Maennel who defected and testified at the trials of **Kauffman** and **Borger**. (AFOSI Investigative Case File)

(RIGHT-Figure 22) KGB officer Chernyshev, who was detained in Queens, New York City, with James Wood. Wood had been paid $1,000 through a dead drop in California prior to his trip to New York to meet with Chernyshev. (AFOSI Investigative Case File)

Illustration

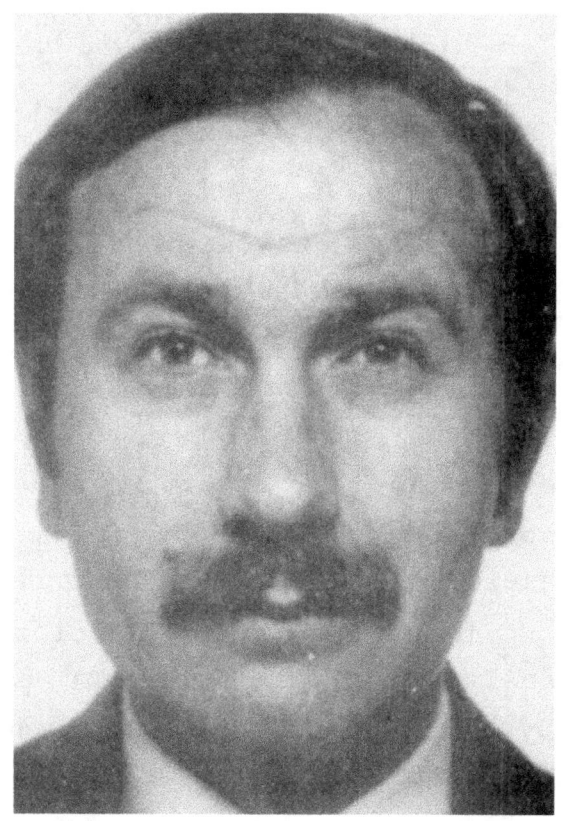

(Figure 23) GRU Colonel Izmaylov, who was declared persona non grata after being detained by AFOSI and FBI agents at a dead drop in rural Maryland where he was hoping to retrieve classified information pertaining to the Strategic Defense Initiative (SDI) program. When detained, Colonel Izmaylov claimed that he was looking for a fishing spot. His fishing tackle box was empty. Earlier in the evening he had loaded a dead drop for an Air Force office containing $8,000, special film, and future clandestine meet instructions. Generally, Soviet tradecraft practices require that the case officer unload the espionage agents dead drop first and retrieve the classified information before loading a dead drop with money and instructions. (AFOSI Investigative Case File)

Chapter 4

PATTERNS AND TRENDS

> A lot of people we're getting now were in college during the Vietnam era, when it was OK to be disloyal to your Government.
>
> **unnamed security official
> at defense plant in California**

In previous chapters, the nature of espionage in the Air Force was discussed in terms of how the hostile intelligence services spotted, assessed, and recruited USAF personnel to become espionage agents, or handled them once they volunteered their services. Additionally, the nature of espionage in the Air Force was examined in regard to how the hostile intelligence services communicated with their espionage agent through clandestine methods.

In this chapter, espionage in the Air Force will be analyzed from a different perspective--the traitor himself. By examining and comparing the backgrounds and characteristics of Air Force personnel known to be involved in espionage, we will be able to better understand their motivating factors and to determine if there are any patterns or trends which may be exploited by offensive or defensive counterespionage programs.

Environmental factors are used most frequently as an explanation of crime or of its causes. Espionage is a criminal offense, committed by persons with confused social values. Examining the environment of Air Force traitors disclosed some interesting patterns and trends, but no conclusive method for identifying people who may later commit espionage.

Patterns and Trends

A person's environment--the time, place, and conditions of life--is rarely unique, that is, a great many other people live in similar environments, yet do not become involved in criminal or other antisocial behavior. There is no simple explanation for crime, and in particular, espionage. The reasons that individuals steal, rob, kill, cheat, engage in extra-marital affairs, abuse narcotics, or spy are numerous and varied. Therefore, the most practical way to learn about traitors is to examine environmental factors and analyze individual investigative case histories.

People who deviate from the norms of society usually rationalize their deviance, unless they are psychotic--and traitors are not. Rationalizations for deviance may be difficult to maintain when the deviance leads to suffering and a sense of failure or guilt, unless there is exceptionally strong support for the deviance from others.[1]

Traitors receive support from their case officers. The Soviet case officer may sooth his agents feelings by talking in terms of world peace, freedom, or the good of mankind; he may pretend to be a traitor's best friend (but in reality, and particularly with mercenary traitors, the KGB and GRU officers will be disgusted with the traitor) by solving problems, listening, and showing the traitor a "night on the town" if needed to keep his spirits up.

In simple terms, a good case officer will quickly sense his agents self-doubts or misgivings and be prepared to exploit the traitor's ego and personality to keep him or her ensnared in espionage. If the traitor is seeking adventure and thrill, then the case officer may become more

Volunteers

conspiratorial than need be. The case officer usually can ease the traitor's doubts and assist the rationalization process by simply promising more money and if absolutely necessary to actually pay more money. If deviant pursuits (treason) are persistently gratifying (excitement, adventure, thrill, money), most tendencies toward nondeviant behavior will soon disappear.

As noted in Chapter 1, the majority of USAF personnel who became involved in espionage were volunteers. In these cases, the USAF member took a positive step to establish contact with the hostile intelligence service. In seven cases,* this involved simply walking into an official establishment to make contact. Writing or telephoning an official establishment occurred in seven cases, and establishing personal contact in some other manner accounted for eight.**

In 18 cases--the overwhelming majority--money is considered to be the primary reason for committing espionage. Ideological motivation can be found in only one case, that of **Ahadi** (Chapter 5) and, surprisingly, she was not motivated by Marxist-Leninist theory or Communism, but by

---

*In 16 of 23 cases (69.7 percent), the initial approach was made overseas. Initial contact with the hostile intelligence service overseas tended to be more successful (from the traitor's point of view) than contacts made in the United States. GRUNDEN, FRENCH, BUCHANAN, OTT, COOKE, DAVIES, and WOOD, were all detected and apprehended shortly after they attempted to commit espionage.

**In one case, a USAF spy made contact for his accomplice, and in another, it has not been determined how initial contact was made.

strong political-nationalistic feelings toward her husband's homeland--the United Arab Republic (UAR)--which were intensified after Israel defeated Egypt in the 1967 war.

Kauffman (Chapter 5) appeared to be sympathetic to communism because of his brother's influence, but his motivation cannot be considered "ideological" in the true meaning of the word. His sympathy, however, may have made it easier to rationalize the involvement and reduce the internal emotional stress resulting from betrayal of your country for money.

Revenge and disaffection as motivation to commit espionage were the primary reasons offered by **Thompson**, **Walton**, and, most recently, **Davies**. However, both **Thompson** and **Walton** requested and received money for their betrayal. **Davies** sought revenge for what he believed was unfair treatment. He had been discharged from the USAF for poor duty performance and drug abuse.

Adventurism and ego-centered personalities were primary motivating factors for **Cooke, Mueller,** and **Wood**, although both **Cooke** and **Wood** had monetary interests as a strong secondary motive. Both **Cooke** and **Wood** also had strong desires to live out fantasies of being involved in clandestine activities; in addition, they were seeking the "adventure" of female companionship. **Wood** was searching for extra-marital relationships; **Cooke** was searching for relationships with "older foreign women."

DeChamplain claimed that Soviet intelligence officers blackmailed him because of a homosexual relationship with his Thai brother-in-law, as well as threatening his parents residing in the United States. As noted in Chapter 2, **DeChamplain's** real motivation centered on solving his financial problems.

Perkins also said that he was blackmailed and he appears to be the only USAF individual who could make this assertion with some truthfulness. Although, **Perkins** may have become a traitor because of coercion from Soviet Intelligence; he appears to have become "hooked" on the excitement of being involved in a clandestine relationship, as well as financial incentives provided by the GRU. Other traitors have also remarked about the thrill and adventure of committing espionage. A powerful psychological attachment develops which just reinforces the deviant behavior similar to the psychological dependency found among drug and alcohol abusers.

Although money was the most frequent motivating factor in USAF espionage case histories, it is interesting to note that not all USAF spies had financial problems. **Boeckenhaupt, Buchanan, Cascio, Jones, Crest, Cooke,** and **Borger** all appeared to have been living within their financial means and were just greedy or wanted to improve their lifestyles. These traitors knew that the hostile intelligence services sometimes paid for classified information and exploited their access to information for financial gain.

In contrast, financial difficulties appear to be at the center of motivation for **DeChamplain, French, Grunden, Ott, Perkins, Thompson,** and **Wood**. **Bronson, Grunden, Perkins, Thompson,** and **Wood** were attempting to support expensive extra-marital affairs; however, only one wife was known to have continually complained of a lack of money.

DeChamplain was having a homosexual affair with his brother-in-law, as well as attempting to support more than 20 friends and relatives.

Bronson became involved in espionage to solve his financial troubles, but surprisingly it appears that he did not use any of the payments received from the GRU for this purpose. It is interesting to note that many of those individuals with financial problems were having extra-marital affairs and were all known to be heavy drinkers and carousers.

According to the FBI, of the various tactics used by hostile intelligence officers, those geared to exploit an American's material needs are perhaps the most common and effective. Many Soviet and other Communist intelligence officers believe that Americans, as capitalists, are hopeless materialists who can be swayed by appeals to greed. In the early 1960's, a Western intelligence service obtained a copy of a KGB training manual used to teach new officers prior to assignment in the United States. The following is a direct quotation from the manual:[2]

> The successful use of financial motivation in recruitment requires above all an understanding of the psychological make-up of the average American. He seriously regards money as the only thing which can ensure his personal freedom and independence and make it possible for him to satisfy his material and spiritual needs. This typical American attitude toward money creates indifference to the means by which it is obtained, even though risk is sometimes involved.

Volunteers

In a recent survey of 200,000 college students by the American Council of Education, over 75 percent admitted that financial reward was their reason for attending college. In a simliar survey 20 years ago, only 39 percent were motivated by money. The desire to get rich quick among traitors (as well as many young Americans) is contrary to the beliefs held by young Americans and the ideological traitors of the 1930's and 1940's.[3]

During 1949-73, there were 16 USAF personnel known to be involved in espionage (Figures 24 and 25). With the exception of **Grunden**, **Boeckenhaupt**, and **Mueller**, all of the remaining traitors who were active during this period were approaching middle age and had substantial years of military or Federal service completed at the time of their recruitment (Figure 24). Since 1973, there were seven spies detected; their ages ranged from 21 to 33. With the exception of **Bronson** and **Davies**, they all had just begun their military careers. Although the data base is too small to draw any solid conclusion, when comparing past cases with recent ones, it does appear that, in general, USAF spies are younger and have completed brief periods of military service.

In the case of **Buchanan** it appears that he intended to commit espionage at the outset of his military career and at the time of his apprehension his security clearance had not been fully adjudicated! The apparent trend between age and monetary gain is interesting. Air Force traitors have always been interested in money, but in cases from 1949 to 1973, the betrayal did not begin until the traitor was reaching the end

Figure 24

AGE WHEN ESPIONAGE BEGAN

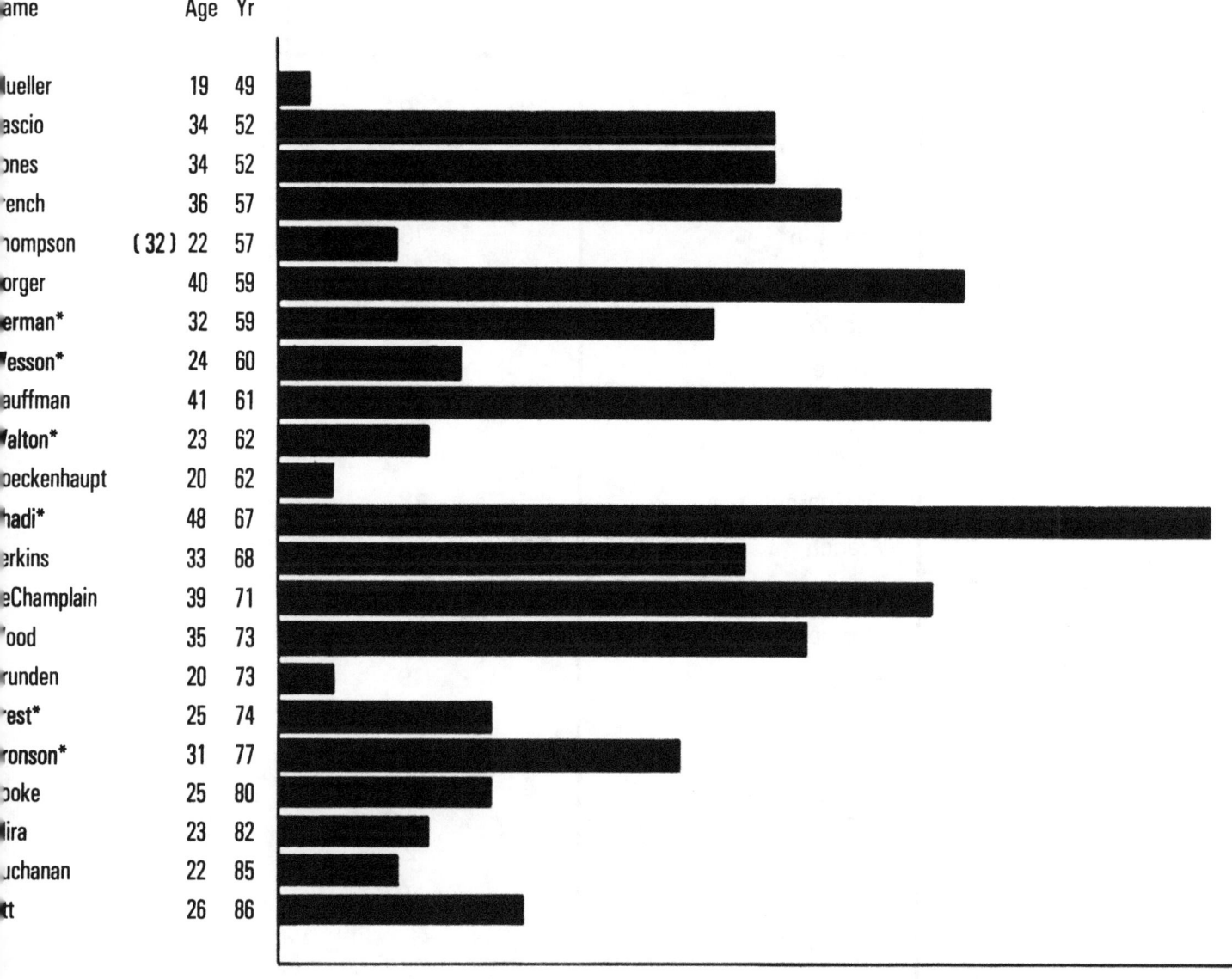

Trends Analysis

* PSEUDONYMS

Figure 25

YEARS OF FEDERAL SERVICE WHEN UNCOVERED

Name	Years
Ahadi*	25
Boeckenhaupt	7
Borger	12
Bronson*	13
Buchanan	1
Cascio	9
Cooke	1
Crest*	3
Davies	10
DeChamplain	18
French	15
Grunden	1
Herman*	16
Kauffman	19
Jones	9
Mira	3
Mueller	1
Ott	2
Perkins	19
Thompson	8
Wesson*	6
Walton*	10
Wood	18

*   PSEUDONYMS

of his or her career. With the shifting values in American society ("live for today," "the me generation," and "get rich quick") it appears that societal values are being reflected in today's breed of Air Force traitor. The older traitors may have had some feelings of disgruntlement or realization that life had passed them by. For them treachery may have been nothing more than a symptom of alienation from society. If they felt society had passed them by or rejected them, they, in turn, may have felt it was right to reject society. **Kauffman**, **Wood**, **Walton**, **Thompson**, and **Herman** all are typical examples.

Younger traitors may also feel alienated, but treachery for them appears to be centered around a failure to understand and accept social beliefs of loyalty, patriotism, and other positive social values.

In reviewing the marital status and influence of foreign family members or friends (Figure 26), there appear to be some commonalities in USAF traitors' backgrounds, but, as noted, the data base is insufficient to draw any definite conclusion. **Boeckenhaupt** married shortly after establishing a clandestine relationship with the GRU, and **Ott** married a few weeks before contacting the Soviets. Fifteen other USAF spies were married, with four divorcing their wives. One individual (**Crest**) is known to have been married to a member of an East Bloc Communist party whose parents were influential Communist party members. **Cascio** married three times, once to his first wife and twice to his second wife. Three of the traitors were unmarried and the marital status of three others is not reflected in available records.

Figure 26

FOREIGN INFLUENCE

Name	Husband	Wife	Mother	Father	Other
Ahadi*	Egyptian		Syrian	Syrian	
Boeckenhaupt		Married	German	American	
Borger		Argentinian	Russian	Austrian	
Bronson*		Japanese	American	American	
Buchanan		Single	American	American	
Cascio		American	Unknown	Unknown	
Cooke		Single	American	American	Indian Girlfriend
Crest*		Hungarian	Hungarian	Hungarian	
Davies		Korean	American	American	
DeChamplain		Thai	American	American	
French		American	American	American	
Grunden		American	American	American	
Herman*		Unknown	Romanian	Romanian	
Kauffman		Single	Russian	Russian	
Jones		Unknown	Unknown	Unknown	
Mira		Single	American	Spanish	German
Mueller		Unknown	English	Swiss	
Ott		American	American	American	
Perkins		Japanese	American	American	
Thompson		German	Russian	German	
Wesson*		German	English	American	
Walton*		American	American	American	
Wood		American	American	American	

* PSEUDONYMS

Seventeen USAF traitors were married, nine of whom had foreign-born wives. In seven cases, both parents of the spy were foreign born; in two, only the mother was foreign; and in one, just the father. In two cases, the traitors had developed strong relationships with their foreign-born girlfriends. Seventeen cases involved the traitors serving at least one tour in an overseas area, and in two others, the spies had traveled to foreign countries.

As noted earlier, several traitors plagued by financial problems had extra-marital affairs, which very likely contributed to their financial predicament. Generally, security officials (as well as banks, employers, insurance companies, and so forth) believe that a married person will have a stabilizing influence in their life and be socially more responsible. This obviously does not hold true when discussing USAF traitors. The heavy influence of foreign spouses, parents, girlfriends, and assignments among USAF traitors provides them a broad, cosmopolitan life-experience which may "muddy the water" in terms of loyalty and patriotism. However, at best, this factor is misleading because thousands of loyal Air Force personnel travel and reside overseas as well as marry and have close relatives and friendships with foreign citizens.

The career fields of or jobs held by USAF members involved in espionage were also examined (Figure 27). There were five career fields from which more than one person became involved in espionage: two of these (Intelligence and Administrative) accounted for 11 cases, the remaining three

Figure 27

CAREER FIELDS OF TRAITORS

Name	Career Field
Ahadi*	Intelligence Analyst
Boeckenhaupt	Communications (Crypto-Repairman)
Borger	Unknown
Bronson*	Communications (Signals Intercept)
Buchanan	Munitions
Cascio	Photo Lab Technician
Cooke	Missile Launch Officer
Crest*	Transportation (Driver)
Davies	Aircraft Maintenance (C-130)
DeChamplain	Administrative
French	Aircrew (Navigator)
Grunden	Aircraft Maintenance (U-2)
Herman*	Intelligence Specialist
Kauffman	Finance Officer
Jones	Unknown
Mira	Communications
Mueller	Intelligence Specialist
Ott	Administrative (SR-71)
Perkins	Intelligence Specialist
Thompson	Administrative (Counterintelligence)
Wesson*	Aircrew (Radio Operator)
Walton*	Administrative (Personnel)
Wood	Counterintelligence

* PSEUDONYMS

(Communications, Aircrew, and Maintenance) accounted for two cases each.

As expected, the intelligence career field had the highest number of traitors. Foreign intelligence services have historically targeted the intelligence services of their enemies, expending considerable resources to penetrate their opposition. The KGB has a specific section which has a main function of recruiting and penetrating opposition intelligence services. In Moscow, this section is part of the First Chief Directorate and is known as Directorate K, which supervises intelligence officers in the field and is responsible for penetrating opposition intelligence and security services. These field officers are assigned to the section known as Line KR.

Four of six USAF members involved in espionage while assigned to intelligence-related jobs were known to have initiated contact with hostile intelligence services and there is strong evidence that **Perkins** also initiated contact. They all knew that the Soviets would be willing to pay for classified information; in addition, they knew where to go and who to contact. Both the only ideological traitor and the only traitor who may have been blackmailed came from intelligence duty assignments.

Individuals assigned to administrative jobs have also provided the Soviets with exploitable targets. At first thought, administrative clerks and secretaries would not seem lucrative targets, but just the opposite is true. They often have much greater access to a wide variety of classified

Volunteers

information, sometimes more than the managers and project officers for whom they work. In general, such workers are responsible for the accounting, mailing, and destruction of classified information. They also are less well paid and thus more susceptible to financial difficulties. The hostile intelligence services recognize the potential of exploiting low-ranking administrative clerks and secretaries.* Of the five USAF administrative clerks who became involved in espionage, one had access to counterintelligence information; another had access to Top Secret military-political and intelligence information; and a third had extensive access to personnel records, worldwide manpower statistics, and base locations.

As Figure 27 illustrates, the only commonalities among any of these traitors in regard to their duty assignments is that they all had access to classified information (with the exception of **Buchanan**), official information which would have been of interest, or knowledge of USAF personnel with character weaknesses who ultimately could be exploited. In simple terms, any military or Government official who approaches a foreign intelligence service may be accepted as an espionage agent, at least initially until the hostile intelligence service can determine if the person is a legitimate traitor or a provocation by counterintelligence. Obviously, the more current and sensitive the information, the more likely the hostile intelligence service will be

---

*Historically, the East German Intelligence Services have been quite successful in exploitation of administrative and secretarial personnel against their main target--West Germany.

willing to risk becoming involved in a clandestine relationship, as illustrated in the **Bronson** case. Access is the key to successful espionage. When desperate (financial problem, greed, revenge, ego, adventure, and so forth) a person with access may commit espionage instead of some other antisocial act.

A review of educational records (Figure 28) revealed that the overwhelming majority (21) had high school diplomas. In addition, one earned an associate's degree; three earned bachelor of science degrees; and one earned a master's degree. Seven others had accumulated college credits, ranging from less than a year to more than 3 years. In contrast, there was one high school dropout. There is no evidence directly linking educational status with these cases, but it is interesting to note that many of the traitors were described by peers and coworkers as being "intelligent," "shrewd," and "cunning." Although most appeared to be educated, intelligent, and sensible, their actions concerning espionage often seemed to have been foolhardy or not well planned. Some sociologists believe that there is a correlation between educational status and a person's beliefs and acceptance of societal standards. As with foreign influence, education may influence some people to be more cosmopolitan and open to a variety of ideas, but again, this factor must be coupled with several others to be meaningful when examining the problem of espionage.

Figure 28

EDUCATIONAL BACKGROUNDS

Name	Education
Ahadi*	College, 2 years
Boeckenhaupt	High School Graduate
Borger	Some College
Bronson*	Some College
Buchanan	High School Graduate
Cascio	High School Graduate
Cooke	Master's Degree
Crest*	High School Graduate
Davies	Some College
DeChamplain	High School Graduate
French	High School Graduate
Grunden	High School Graduate
Herman*	Associate's Degree
Kauffman	Bachelor's Degree
Jones	Unknown
Mira	High School Graduate
Mueller	Some College
Ott	High School Graduate
Perkins	Some College
Thompson	High School Dropout
Wesson*	Some College
Walton*	Bachelor's Degree
Wood	Bachelor's Degree

* PSEUDONYMS

Patterns and Trends

Considering that money was the primary reason for committing espionage in the majority of cases, USAF spies were not well paid (Figure 29). The classified information obtained by the Soviets was bought at bargain prices. **Boeckenhaupt** ($16,000), **Walton** ($18,000), and **Wesson** ($13,000) were paid the largest sums, but they all betrayed the USAF for several years. When taking into account the number of years **Thompson** betrayed the USAF and the value of the information he provided to the KGB, he obviously was underpaid at $4,000. **DeChamplain** ($3,800) and **Wood** ($1,000) were detected shortly after they started to spy which is why their remuneration was small. After contacting the GRU, **Bronson** ($950) lost his access to classified information and, ironically, if the Soviets had paid him more money initially, he may have avoided losing his security clearance. **Cooke** was paid a token $50 (the Soviets never really believed he was a legitimate spy, but rather a likely provocation by U.S. counterintelligence), and **Kauffman** neither asked for, nor received, any money. It is unknown how much was paid (if any) to **Ahadi, Borger, Crest, Herman,** or **Perkins**. **Perkins** claimed not to have received any money except reimbursement for expenses; however, this undoubtedly was not true because he spent money lavishly, and invested in a bar in Tokyo, Japan. **Cascio, Buchanan, Davies, French, Grunden, Jones, Mueller,** and **Ott** were all apprehended by counterintelligence officers before providing any classified information to a hostile intelligence service. **French, Ott, Buchanan,** and **Cascio** all asked for money; **Cooke** admitted

77

Figure 29

MONIES RECEIVED BY TRAITORS

Name	Payment
Ahadi*	Unknown
Boeckenhaupt	$15,000 - $16,000
Borger	Unknown
Bronson*	$950
Buchanan	None
Cascio	None
Cooke	$50
Crest*	Unknown
Davies	None
DeMira	$1,900
DeChamplain	$3,800
French	None
Grunden	None
Herman*	Unknown
Kauffman	Did not Request Any
Jones	None
Mira	$1,900
Mueller	None
Ott	None
Perkins	Unknown
Thompson	$4,000
Wesson*	$13,000
Walton*	$18,000
Wood	$1,000

* PSEUDONYMS

that he was going to ask for $3,000. For comparison, Figure 30 highlights several recent cases of espionage and what these traitors were paid.[4]

The basic social institution is the home; and it is with the family, particularly in the early years, that personality traits, social values, and qualities of adulthood are developed. General agreement exists among most criminologists and sociologists that a good home environment will lead to proper acceptance of social responsibilities. However, even good homes may provide an avenue for antisocial tendencies to develop. Where there is divorce, immorality, or criminality, there is likely to be more criminality or antisocial behavior among children and young adults. Unfortunately, investigative case files provide little insight in terms of the traitors' home environment. One factor which can be examined, however, is the effect of the broken home, either through divorce or death of a parent.

For a child, death or separation from his or her parents is a particularly traumatic experience and this occurrence has been cited as the cause of many sociological and psychological adjustment problems later on as an adult. It has been estimated that broken homes cause 30 to 50 percent of juvenile delinquency.

The early death of a parent, or separation from one or both parents, occurred in 50 percent of the childhoods of USAF traitors. **Cooke** and **Mueller's** fathers were murdered; **Thompson's** father died when **Thompson** was 6 years old; **Herman's** entire family was exterminated by the

Figure 30

MONIES RECEIVED BY NON-USAF TRAITORS

Name	Age	Year	Payment
Boyce, Christopher TRW Code Clerk	23	73	$15,000
Cavanaugh, Thomas Northrup Engineer	40	84	$25,000 (Briefly)
Chin, Larry Wu-Tai CIA Analyst	63	52-84	$180,000+
Kampiles, William CIA Watch Officer	23	78	$3,000
Lee, Andrew Friend of Boyce	25	77	$53,000
Miller, Richard FBI Agent	47	84	$40.00 (Note 1)
Pelton, Ronald NSA Computer Specialist	44	80-85	$35,000 (Note 2)
Pollard, Anne Wife of Jonathan	25	84-85	(Note 3)
Pollard, Jonathan Navy Intel Analyst	31	84-85	$45,000
Walker, John Navy Comm Specialist	47	68-85	$1 million
Walker, Michael Navy Seaman	21	84-85	$5,000
Whitworth, Jerry Navy Code Clerk	45	75-85	$332,000

Note 1 - Also given Italian shoes, jogging suit, gym bag, and cap.

Note 2 - In addition, Pelton received travel expenses.

Note 3 - Husband gave her $1,000 diamond and sapphire ring.

Nazis in a concentration camp at the end of World War II; and **Kauffman's** parents died when he was quite young, and afterwards he lived with 15 foster parents. **Boeckenhaupt, Cascio, Wesson,** and **Crest** all had parents who divorced. Additionally, **Boeckenhaupt's** father became a Nazi and is believed to have physically abused his wife and son.[5] Although there appears to be a high percentage of death or separation of parents during the childhoods of individuals who later joined the USAF and became involved in espionage, there is no evidence to support any direct link to treachery.

Undoubtedly, as noted, these individuals had traumatic childhood experiences, but these experiences alone do not make a person more susceptible to becoming involved in espionage or any type of criminal activity. Among social scientists, criminologists, and psychologists, there is a general belief that the divorce or the death of a parent may contribute to antisocial behavior, but this theory alone cannot explain why a handful of individuals elect to commit espionage instead of some other antisocial action. In fact, many who suffer traumatic experiences or come from broken homes become exemplary citizens.

Other commonalities in USAF spies' experiences, behavioral patterns, and personalities are also difficult to link directly to their involvement in espionage. Seven were born of "lower-middle class" parents and entered the service at an early age. Poor civilian job prospects seems to have been the reason for joining the Air Force in many cases.

Only two sexual deviants can be found in these case histories (although there were a few others where homosexuality was suspected). **DeChamplain** and his wife separated early in their marriage and he chose instead to live with her brother in a homosexual relationship; **Ott** engaged in homosexual acts with his priest.

In several cases, such as **Buchanan**, **DeChamplain**, and **Ott**, the traitor told stories to explain their anticipated monetary affluence. As noted earlier, six traitors worked in the intelligence career field and had extensive knowledge of hostile intelligence service activities, and tradecraft. At least three other traitors (**Cooke, Buchanan, and Ott**) had read a "spy" book prior to their involvement in espionage. **DeChamplain, Perkins, and Ahadi** were known to have falsified classified destruction certificates.

One final characteristic frequently found among traitors is known as the "pack rat syndrome." To be successful at espionage, a traitor must acquire documents of interest to the hostile intelligence service. As a result, many tend to stockpile documents long before making contact with a hostile intelligence service. **Cooke, Wood, and Perkins** are typical examples of this tendency.

In general, some USAF members involved in treason could be described as being rather moody, self-indulgent, and sexually promiscuous. Most are weak-willed persons having trouble coping with the pressures and responsibilities of their personal and professional lives.[6] Contrary to popular belief, few, if any, of them were loners. Although many had difficulties in forming long-lasting relationships, they did develop social acquaintances and friends, as well as meet, date, and marry.

Patterns and Trends

This chapter was intended to provide a brief description of the patterns and trends of espionage in the USAF. In the final chapter, detailed summaries of each espionage case is provided for those wishing to have a more indepth appreciation for the backgrounds and characteristics of USAF espionage agents.

Chapter 5

CASE SUMMARIES

The soul of the spy is somehow the model of us all.
                    Jacques Barzun

Introduction

The following case summaries provide pertinent details of USAF personnel (both military and civilian) who engaged in espionage or attempted to establish an espionage relationship with a foreign government. These summaries, arranged alphabetically by last name, are not limited only to those cases which resulted in a successful prosecution. They also encompass a few cases in which the suspect was not prosecuted, either in an effort to protect a sensitive source or because of a lack of evidence.

Although some of the cases were never prosecuted, there is little (if any) doubt that the suspect was acting as an espionage agent for a foreign government. These case summaries provide the reader with enough detailed information to draw their own conclusions as to the degree of involvement a suspect had with a foreign intelligence service. The student of espionage or the professional counterintelligence officer will not only find these case summaries interesting, but also extremely useful in future analysis or comparison with other espionage case histories.

For the first time, all of the known subject USAF espionage cases are discussed in one unclassified study designed to provide accurate and definitive reference material for the counterintelligence analyst or security officer.

Case Summaries

For many students and professionals alike, these case summaries will hopefully dispel the myths and rumors which have abounded concerning the nature of espionage in the Air Force.

Figure 31

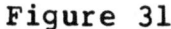

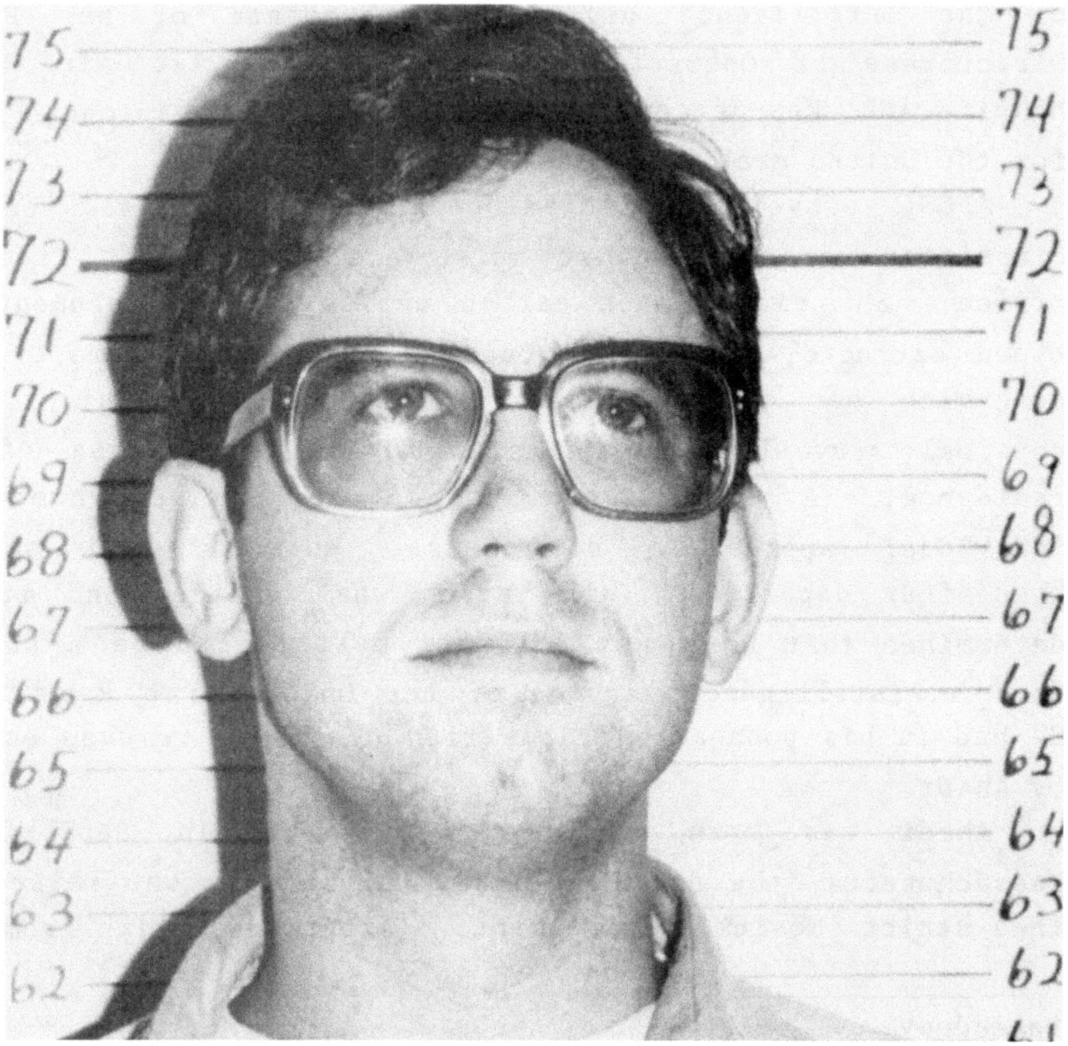

2Lt **Christopher Cooke**, a Titan Missile launch officer was apprehended after contacting Soviet officials on several occasions and providing them with handwritten notes and photographs of classified information. He was paid $50 by the Soviets before he was arrested. (AFOSI Investigative Case File)

Volunteers

Ahadi*

Mrs. **Ahadi**, a Department of the Air Force (DAF) civilian intelligence analyst (GS-11), assigned as the Chief of the Intelligence Division, Directorate of War Plans, Directorate of Operations and Plans, HQ 21st Air Force, McGuire AFB, New Jersey, was identified as an espionage agent for the United Arab Republic (UAR).

AFOSI surveillance disclosed that **Ahadi** was putting classified material in her purse and removing it from the office. She either kept carbon copies of the documents or typed extracts, and then brought these to her home. After observing her remove classified material in this manner physical surveillance was established in the area of her residence. A short time after she arrived home, an individual approached her house, entered, and shortly thereafter departed. This person was detained and it was determined that he was a student, believed to be a courier for the intelligence service of the United Arab Republic.** He had in his possession classified documents removed earlier by **Ahadi**.[1]

Ahadi was born on March 23, 1918 in Springfield, Massachusetts, the daughter of Syrian parents who raised her in a strict Moslem environment. After graduating from high

---

*pseudonym

** The United Arab Republic (Egypt) and the United States severed diplomatic relations in June 1967.

school in 1934, working at various odd jobs, and attending college (but not receiving a degree), she entered government service, initially starting as a clerk stenographer for the Director of Intelligence (A-2), HQ Army Air Force, Washington, DC. She spent her entire career in the intelligence field, working her way up through the ranks, from stenographer, administrative assistant, research analyst, intelligence officer, and finally to Chief of an Intelligence Division.

In 1948, she married a naturalized Egyptian who worked as a warehouseman at McGuire AFB from 1955 until 1967. Her Top Secret security clearance was granted in 1952. In 1965, she was reprimanded for committing a security violation. She signed a destruction certificate as a witness, when she did not actually observe the document's destruction.[2]

Ahadi and her husband were vehemently anti-Jewish, pro-Egyptian, and, in particular, pro-Nasser (then the President of Egypt). The couple traveled to Egypt on several occasions and had numerous friends and relatives throughout the Arab world. It is believed that she volunteered her services to the UAR through already-established social contacts, and she claimed her involvement in espionage started as a result of the Israeli victory in the 1967 Yom Kippur war. She claimed only to have provided extracts of three classified documents (one Secret and two Confidential) and two unclassified documents. These all were intelligence documents she felt would be of interest to the UAR.[3]

Volunteers

Ahadi was not prosecuted, but she was allowed to retire on medical grounds; a psychiatric examination revealed that she was suffering from a minor psychological disorder.[4]

Herbert W. Boeckenhaupt

SSgt Herbert W. Boeckenhaupt, a communications specialist and crypto-repairman, assigned to the 33rd Communications Squadron, March AFB, California, was observed meeting on two occasions with Aleksey R. Malinin, a GRU officer assigned to the Soviet Military Mission in Washington, DC. Malinin was operating under diplomatic cover as the Assistant Commercial Attache.[5] **Boeckenhaupt** was apprehended by AFOSI on October 24, 1966 in Riverside, California.[6]

Born on November 26, 1942 in Mannheim, Germany, the first of three children, and the son of an American father and German mother, **Boeckenhaupt** was raised in a German, lower middle-class environment before moving in 1947 to Superior, Wisconsin with his mother when his parents separated. **Boeckenhaupt's** natural father elected to remain in Germany after the war and eventually lost his U.S. citizenship because of his belief in Nazism.*

---

*At the time of his son's arrest for espionage, Mr. Boeckenhaupt scoffed at charges that his son was involved in espionage and referred to himself as "a notorious anti-communist" when questioned by reporters (<u>Newsweek</u>, Nov. 14, 1966).

With no real job prospects, **Boeckenhaupt** enlisted in the USAF at age 17 on July 28, 1960, after completing the 11th grade. Boeckenhaupt became a model airman and had no serious weaknesses which could be exploited, except that he liked to spend money freely. Shortly after starting his espionage career, he married a woman from Maryland who lived near Andrews AFB.[7]

While stationed in Mississippi, prior to his transfer to Morocco, **Boeckenhaupt** claimed he developed an idea to contact the Soviets and commit espionage. Boeckenhaupt did not attempt to contact the Soviets while in the United States.[8] In October 1962, he purposely traveled to Rabat, Morocco and walked into the Soviet Embassy, volunteering his services. From October 1962 to July 1963, **Boeckenhaupt** had numerous personal meetings and dead drops with the GRU in Morocco. During this period, he furnished photographs of all information or documents available to him from the communications site at his base in Sidi Slimane, Morocco, inflicting considerable damage to the security of USAF communication systems. He received between $11,000 and $12,000, as well as instructions for initiating and maintaining contact with the Soviets after he was reassigned to the United States.[9]

In July 1963, **Boeckenhaupt** was assigned to Carswell AFB, Texas, but managed to have his assignment changed to the 2045 Communications Group, Andrews AFB, Maryland. He continued to communicate with the Soviets via dead drops and had several personal meetings with GRU officer

Volunteers

Malinin.* Boeckenhaupt claims not to have passed any information during this period; however, the Soviets paid him $4,000.

In August 1965, **Boeckenhaupt** was transferred to Lackland AFB, Texas. He was equipped with an accommodation address in London and secret writing materials so that he could schedule meetings with Malinin in Washington, DC. While attending a crypto training course at Lackland AFB, he attempted to manipulate an assignment to the Pentagon because he believed it would be more valuable to the Soviets (earning him more money); however, he was reassigned to March AFB, California. Although claiming not to have passed any information to the Soviets, he remained in contact during this period sending letters with secret writing to the London accommodation address.

According to Newsweek, 2 days after **Boeckenhaupt's** arrest, British authorities arrested Cecil William Mulvena, a 47-year-old real estate agent with dual French-British citizenship for violating the British Official Secrets Act. According to press reports, Mulvena, who resided in Southend-on-Sea, London, was believed to be the accommodation address keeper where **Boeckenhaupt** sent secret writing messages to be forwarded to the GRU. For example, on 20 April 1966, he used this method to arrange a meeting with

---

*For example, **Boeckenhaupt** and Malinin conducted their second personal meeting in a Fairfax County, Virginia bowling alley parking lot. **Boeckenhaupt's** arrest in 1966 was the fourth major case in the United States and all suspects met their Soviet case officers in parking lots and restaurants in the Washington, DC area (Time, November 1966, p.33.)

Malinin in Alexandria, Virginia. Malinin gave him $1,500 and a film clip containing future meet instructions; he was also told to continue to use the accommodation address in London. **Boeckenhaupt** was also provided with an accommodation address in Bangkok, Thailand.[10] A search of his residence in Riverside, California disclosed secret writing paper, as well as clandestine instructions for personal meetings and dead drops. The personal meet and dead drop instructions were contained on a 35mm negative.[11]

Boeckenhaupt claimed that immaturity, coupled with a passover for promotion which he felt he deserved, led him to the idea of committing espionage. Although his real motivation was strictly monetary, he was not in any financial difficulty. In a word, "greed" was the motivation. His desire for money was his motivation to remain in contact with the Soviets.

Boeckenhaupt provided the Soviet Union with code and signal books, maps, instruments, sketches, and photographs. Convicted in 1967 on two counts of conspiring to commit espionage, he received a 30-year sentence from Judge Oren R. Lewis. When imposing sentence, Judge Lewis told **Boeckenhaupt** that his crimes "were the most heinous I can think of."[12]

Harold Noah Borger

In May 1962, a German court sentenced **Harold Noah Borger** to serve 2-1/2 years in prison for violation of the German Penal Code and the Status of Forces of Agreement when he attempted to obtain classified military information for the East German Intelligence Service (EGIS).[13]

Borger, the son of Jewish emigres (his mother was born in Odessa, Russia, and his father in Austria), was born on July 4, 1919 in New York City.[14] After graduating from high school and attending several colleges (including George Washington University in Washington, DC), he was inducted into the Army Air Force on August 8, 1941, receiving a commission in November 1942. He was released from active duty on March 5, 1946; however, at his request he was recalled to active duty with the USAF at Bolling AFB, Washington, DC, in August 1946. In 1950, he married an Argentinian woman, but was divorced 3 or 4 years later.[15]

Borger entered the Air Force Reserves and was eventually promoted to the rank of Major. In June 1957, he was discharged as a result of "statements, actions, and membership in Communist fronts and demonstration of subversive activities." He had expressed Communist sympathies, as well as a dislike for the United States, and was known to have received literature from a proscribed organization known to be a Communist front.

From the time of his discharge until his arrest in 1961, **Borger's** activities could best be described as those of a confidence man. Always on the lookout for ways of making a quick dollar, he was involved in several business ventures, traveling to Europe and the Far East--always one step ahead of angered business partners or the law.

Borger was arrested on March 3, 1961, by Army counterintelligence officers after trying to obtain classified military information from a soldier who had reported Borger's request and was working under the direction of Army counterintelligence. Borger was in possession of a classified manual concerning nuclear weapons which he had just received from the soldier working for counterintelligence.[16] He was known to have posed as a USAF Major in an effort to meet servicemen and had requested information and equipment from several other soldiers while in West Germany.

While testifying in court, he admitted that his espionage career began in late 1959, after traveling to Moscow on a business trip. During the trip, he met an East German representative of a domestic and foreign trade organization, who invited him to East Berlin. While in East Berlin, he was approached by a woman, who (according to Borger) told him she worked with Israeli Intelligence and requested his assistance through espionage.

Under interrogation, he claimed that he had collected information, but not for an intelligence service. Borger stated that he hated war and was gathering information so that he could write a book. When questioned about the equipment he was also attempting to obtain, he stated that he was going to evaluate the equipment, see if he could reproduce it, and sell it to the Army at a lower price than what they were currently paying.

Volunteers

In court, Borger described himself as "a gregarious person who was not a trained espionage officer, but who stupidly got involved."[17] The surprise and highlight of the trial occurred when First Lieutenant Gunther Maennel, a former EGIS intelligence officer who had defected to the West in 1961 testified, saying that he had met Borger while Borger had been on one of many trips to East Berlin. Maennel said he attempted to recruit Borger to commit espionage for the EGIS. To Maennel's surprise, Borger told him he could not spy for Maennel, because he was already working for EGIS![18]

A month earlier, Maennel was the star witness at the trial of USAF Captain Kauffman who was also convicted of espionage. Maennel provided the lead which had resulted in the detection of Kauffman and in all probability, had identified Borger to counterintelligence authorities as well. After Maennel's testimony, Borger admitted that his story of being recruited by Israeli Intelligence was just a pretense.

In sentencing Borger, the judge stated that the Israeli Intelligence story was just an excuse by Borger, so that his life would be easier when he returned to the United States.[19] According to the judge, he imposed a light sentence on Borger because Borger's attempt at espionage had been "primitive" and he had been caught before he could provide any damaging information to the East Germans.[20]

Bronson*

In the fall of 1978, information was developed that indicated an Air Force person was engaged in espionage on behalf of the GRU. After evaluating the information, AFOSI counterintelligence officers agreed that the suspect was definitely a black American man, who most likely had been raised in the southern part of United States, and was assigned to a base in England. AFOSI initiated an investigation to locate and identify the unknown espionage agent. AFOSI believed that the unknown espionage agent met a GRU Colonel in White City, London, England, in December 1977, and identified himself to the GRU Colonel as (nickname). Initially, 83 possible suspects were identified; however, further investigative action narrowed the field to 20.[21]

After proper legal coordination and approval, AFOSI contacted each of the suspects using a carefully developed ruse. AFOSI investigators immediately identified one of the suspects as the unknown espionage agent by comparing the information developed from the 20 suspects to the information provided by the source. The suspect was positively identified as **Staff Sergeant Bronson**, formerly assigned to the 6950th Electronic Security Squadron, RAF Chicksands, and holding a Top Secret security clearance. At the time of the identification he was working in the base gymnasium after

---

*pseudonym

Volunteers

having been relieved of duties because of his failure to pay financial obligations.

Bronson was born in Huntsville, Alabama on November 2, 1947, the third of four children and had almost 13 years in the USAF when he became involved in espionage. He was known to be a gambler (blackjack, horses, and dogs) and had a chronic history of indebtedness. An intensive investigation had not developed any further evidence, because contact between the GRU and **Bronson** had been broken, most likely because **Bronson** had lost his access to classified information and thus had nothing to sell to the GRU. Because the investigation had not developed any new information, it was decided to resolve the investigation by using a provocation.*

After AFOSI had carefully developed a scenario, **Bronson** was contacted via telephone by an AFOSI agent posing as a Soviet intelligence officer. Using information obtained during the investigation, the "Soviet official" reminded **Bronson** of his involvement in espionage and requested a

---

* The word "provocation" has two meanings for counterintelligence officers. For example, when a counterintelligence service "walks" a controlled agent into a foreign embassy in the hopes that they might start handling him as an espionage agent, it is just one of many types of provocation which could be conducted. A "provocation" can also be conducted against the subject of an espionage allegation. In this case, a provocation is a carefully designed plan (legally approved) to cause the subject of an investigation to respond with a positive action, if he is the actual espionage agent. **Bronson, Borger, Buchanan, Cascio, Davies, French, Grunden, Jones, Mueller,** and **Ott** were all apprehended in this manner.

meeting. **Bronson's** response positively indicated that he had been the person who was working as an espionage agent for the GRU.[22]

During several interviews, polygraphs, and other investigative actions by AFOSI, it was ascertained that **Bronson** had been in contact with the GRU and had provided them with two codeword documents classified Secret. These documents provided the Soviets with Electronic Security Command capabilities to monitor communication activities. **Bronson** also provided one other similar codeword document, as well as an unclassified message and alpha roster listing all of the personnel assigned to RAF Chicksands.[23]

Although **Bronson** claimed to have initiated contact with the GRU in December 1977, counterintelligence officers are positive that his first contact with Soviet intelligence occurred in October 1977. This contact was made in an attempt to determine where the Soviet Military Attache office was located.[24] A few days before Christmas and a prior visit to the Soviet Military Mission, London, England, Bronson removed a secret codeword document, 20 to 30 pages in length and several months old, by hiding it in his sock before leaving the building and then placing it in the trunk of his car. He then traveled to London to locate the Soviet Military Mission and volunteer by walking in.

Unable to find the Attache Office, he stopped a British police constable and asked him for directions to the Japanese Embassy (his wife was Japanese), thinking that the Soviets and Japanese may have offices in the same general area. The

Volunteers

police constable gave him a listing with the addresses of all of the embassies in London![25] He found the Soviet Military Mission and, wearing a wool cap and dressed like a Jamaican, walked up to the front door.

He claims to have handed the receptionist, who answered the door, a note stating "I'm in the USAF. Have info of interest to you. Please follow." **Bronson** claims that as he departed the building, a Soviet official followed him and when they reached the street the official indicated to **Bronson** that he should follow him. After walking approximately 30 to 40 minutes, they stopped and sat on a bench in the park. **Bronson** identified himself, provided the unclassified message, and agreed to meet the Soviet later that same day at 1400 hours in White City. According to **Bronson**, the meeting took place and he was paid $300 to $400.

This account by **Bronson**, although generally accurate, appears to be a rationalization on his part to avoid admitting that he initially provided a sensitive classified codeword document. To walk right out of the Military Mission and follow a stranger who just handed them an unclassified document would have been extremely risky on the part of the Soviets. In contrast, if the document offered was a sensitive codeword document of obvious value, the Soviets might have taken the risk. Although **Bronson** denied it, the evidence suggests that the Soviet official willingly followed him because **Bronson** had provided a Secret codeword document.[26]

During the next several months, **Bronson** was handled from London by a known GRU officer. **Bronson** had at least six meetings with the GRU in which he was indoctrinated in Soviet espionage tradecraft and, in turn, he provided the Soviets with another classified codeword document, as well as the unclassified message and base alpha roster. **Bronson** had lost his access to classified material in February 1978 and was passing the unclassified material to the Soviets in the hope of receiving additional money.

Bronson was paid about $950 by the Soviets and trained to use dead drops to communicate clandestinely. At a lengthy personal meeting with his case officer in June 1978, he was provided with a concealment device disguised as a rock (made from clay, string, and plastic), a Minox camera, 20 rolls of film, and an ordinance survey map with signal sites and dead drop locations annotated. He was also given photographs of the dead drop locations; and instructions for the dead drops were noted on three cards. Each card was divided into four sections: one section described where and how to leave documents for the Soviets, the next explained where and how to retrieve money from the Soviets for the documents, and another described the various signals he was to use or observe in loading and unloading the dead drops. **Bronson** kept this card in his wallet until he departed the country when reassigned to the United States.[27] On his way back to RAF Chicksands from this personal meeting, he threw the film out of his car window and later pawned the camera.[28]

Bronson claimed that his idea to commit espionage originated, in December 1977, because of his financial problems and impending discharge. He admitted initiating contact with the Soviets, but ironically did not use any of the money the Soviets provided to pay off his debts. If the Soviets initially had paid him more money and he had paid his debts, he would have been able to retain access to sensitive codeword material and could possibly have continued to provide the Soviets with sensitive information for several more months.

During his interviews, **Bronson** initially denied having been involved in espionage, and was also deceptive during polygraph examinations. After providing a more accurate account of his involvement in espionage, **Bronson** ceased being deceptive during polygraph examinations. He admitted to initiating contact with the GRU by walking into the Soviet Military Attache Office in London and offering them classified material which they accepted. **Bronson** also admitted to stealing the second classified codeword document he provided to the Soviets before his access was terminated.

Although it was obvious he had financial difficulties, where his money was going was less apparent. **Bronson** was known to have been involved in several extra-marital affairs, as well as having in his possession numerous "swinger" magazines, contact addresses, and letters he had either written or received.[29] On the surface he appeared to be a normal, intelligent, outgoing, friendly, well-adjusted, and articulate person; however, underneath he was irrational and embarrassed by his financial difficulties and counseling.

Although **Bronson** cooperated with investigators during his interviews, when the questions started to focus on the critical issues relating to his involvement in espionage with the Soviets, he often yawned and dozed off![30] Bronson also displayed other defensive reactions such as rationalizing and lying.

Bronson was not prosecuted in order to protect sensitive sources, but was administratively discharged by the USAF.

Edward Owen Buchanan

In early May 1985, an AFOSI human source provided information that Airman **Edward O. Buchanan**, a student assigned to the 3463 Munitions and Weapons Maintenance Technical Training Squadron, Lowry AFB, Colorado, telephoned the East German Embassy in Washington, DC, on May 6, 1985. He was attempting to learn if Embassy officials had received a letter he had sent in April 1985. According to the source, it contained an offer by **Buchanan** to commit espionage for the East German Government.

During the telephone conversation, **Buchanan** was told by an Embassy employee that the Embassy was closed and he was instructed to telephone the next day. According to AFOSI's source, **Buchanan** telephoned the East German Embassy on May 7, 1985 as instructed; however, an Embassy employee told **Buchanan** that he couldn't help him. **Buchanan** telephoned the East German Embassy an hour later, requested to speak to the Ambassador, was unsuccessful, and hung up. According to the source, **Buchanan** was irritated with being put off by the East Germans and telephoned the Soviet Consulate located

Volunteers

in San Francisco. He told an official of the Soviet Consulate his name, duty location, and that he was in the USAF. Apparently, **Buchanan** was unable to understand the Soviet official who answered the telephone, so he hung up.[31]

According to the source, on May 9, 1985, **Buchanan** mailed a letter to the Soviet Embassy in Washington, DC, fully identifying himself (name, military organization, duty station, and career speciality).[32] The letter stated that he had information of a scientific and technological nature that he wanted to sell to the Russian Government. He indicated in the letter that he would continue to conduct business with the Soviets if they liked his material.

AFOSI carefully developed a legally approved counterintelligence provocation and contacted **Buchanan** on behalf of the Soviet Intelligence Service. According to the source, **Buchanan** was delighted to have been contacted by the Soviets and followed instructions provided to arrange for a personal meeting. **Buchanan**, believing that he was doing business with Soviet Intelligence Officers, offered to commit espionage and sell classified documents. A lengthy discussion ensued in which **Buchanan** reiterated his desire to sell classified defense information to the Soviet Government. He then sold documents to the "Soviets" (undercover AFOSI/FBI agents) which he claimed were classified Secret and was paid $1,000. A later examination of the documents disclosed that they were copies of unclassified articles from an electronics magazine. **Buchanan** was apprehended immediately after selling the documents to the "Soviets."

Case Summaries

During an interview following his apprehension, **Buchanan** admitted contacting the East German Embassy and the Soviet Consulate and Embassy for the purpose of committing espionage. **Buchanan** admitted that, although he did not have access to classified information at that time (because of his student status), he planned to sell classified information once his clearance had been granted and he was assigned to a base in Germany.[33] **Buchanan** was being processed for a Top Secret - Special Compartmented Information clearance. His intention was to establish a business relationship with the Soviets by selling bogus material to "get my foot in the door" and then later sell classified information.

He admitted that he formed the idea to commit espionage in mid-March 1985, with the objective of becoming rich. **Buchanan** explained to his interviewer that he was going to be assigned to Spangdahlem AB, Germany, and would have access to classified material. His intentions were "to sell as much classified material as he could until he made enough money to live comfortably" and once he did, he planned to "defect and live in southern USSR." He told his interviewer that the last week of the training course he was enrolled in was classified and that he planned to smuggle a camera into the class area to take photographs of Sparrow and Sidewinder missiles, which he could then sell to the Soviets. A witness told AFOSI that **Buchanan** talked about a project (unspecified) which he was going to sell in Europe, because the U.S. Government was not interested in buying it from him.

Volunteers

Buchanan was born in Orlando, Florida on August 7, 1963, and was raised in a white, middle-class family environment. After graduating from high school, his civilian job prospects were limited so he enlisted in the USAF on January 16, 1985. At the time of his apprehension, he was unmarried and had completed approximately 1 year of college. Investigative interviews disclosed that he was very naive and immature. Although he expressed an interest in defecting and living in the Soviet Union, financial gain was his primary motivating factor in committing espionage.

After his arrest and while in confinement prior to his court-martial, Buchanan wrote two letters to Congresswoman Paula Hawkins. They not only provide an interesting look at Buchanan's cognitive process, but also reveal his naivety and immaturity. In the first letter[34] he states:

> I'm in the Air Force and I am 21 years old. Presently I am in jail pending judicial action of some sort, they are not sure which charges. This activity dealt with E. Germany and Russia, but there was nothing classified involved, it was all out of a magazine, plus information I made up. No matter what I did, I believe I should be exiled to an abandoned island, from society, in the S. Pacific. Could this be done? For the sake of society and myself!!! Please help!!!

In the second letter[35] to Congresswoman Hawkins, Buchanan states:

> Mam, would you please help me by getting a discharge from the Air Force before the trial? I could be sent to jail for awhile and feel that the govt is at fault. Also, I am mentally weak and I

> do not believe I could stand jail mentally.
> I realize just how great it is to be free,
> legally. Would you <u>please help me</u>? With a
> <u>discharge please</u>!!! <u>Quickly</u>!!! Before July.

On May 17, 1985 AFOSI conducted a search of **Buchanan's** barracks room. A draft letter he had prepared and addressed to the East Germans was discovered. This letter provides additional insight into **Buchanan's** thought process:

> I am a spy that has found the most well-kept
> secret of the U.S. A secret that could
> destroy the Soviet Union off the globe. It
> could destroy the universe. But 1st allow
> me to intro. myself. I work for CIA, DOD
> and other foreign governments, including the
> USSR and Cuba. Also I have sold much
> information to many different countries. I
> have alot of experience in the work I do.
>
> If you are interested in knowing about this
> system to make E. Germany superior I possess
> diagrams and other material on the subject.
> Please meet me at 1st Fed. Savings Bank of
> Colorado with $12,888.88 in Denver, Co on
> May 9th at 2:30 p.m. in the lobby near the
> front door. I keep myself secretive, so
> carry brown briefcase and a black umbrella.
> I will see you there.

After reading this letter, it is understandable why the East Germans informed **Buchanan** they were unable to help him. He was court-martialed on August 26, 1985, and sentenced to 30 months confinement, reduction to Airman Basic, forfeiture of all pay and allowances, and a dishonorable discharge.

Volunteers

Giuseppe Cascio

On September 21, 1952, Staff Sergeant **Giuseppe Cascio**, a 34-year-old photographic laboratory technican assigned to an airbase in South Korea, was apprehended at the conclusion of an investigation which began in August 1952. Staff Sergeant **John P. Jones** was apprehended with **Cascio**.

Cascio, a resident of Tucson, Arizona, had been a bombardier in World War II, twice earning the Distinguished Flying Cross. In an interview with reporters, **Cascio's** 44-year-old wife stated that she married Cascio in 1948, when he was a lieutenant in the USAF, and divorced him in August 1951, only to remarry in December 1951. Mrs. Cascio claimed that her husband was released as an officer in late 1948, and enlisted as a staff sergeant in 1949. She described her husband as "goofy at times."[36] Dr. Russell S. Wolfe, chief medical officer at the Veterans Administration Hospital in Houston, Texas, described **Cascio** as "a dangerous paranoid" and said "I think that in periods of sanity he is a completely loyal American."[37]

Cascio had tried to sell classified flight test data about the F-86E Sabre jet aircraft to North Korean Intelligence Service (NKIS) officers. After accepting military payment certificates from a Korean civilian for the information, Cascio was promptly apprehended by AFOSI Special Agents. He had received his information from **John P. Jones**, a friend assigned to the same base.[38]

On June 8, 1953, **Cascio** was convicted of conspiracy to pass secrets to Communist agents and was sentenced to 20 years at hard labor and a dishonorable discharge. He was also convicted on 16 charges of having used U.S. military payment certificates illegally.[39] Jones was not prosecuted because he had suffered a nervous breakdown and was deemed incompetent to stand trial.

Christopher M. Cooke

On December 23, 1980, it was learned that an unidentified American had placed a telephone call to Richmond, Virginia from inside the Soviet Embassy in Washington, DC.[40] Christopher Cooke, a Second Lieutenant Titan missile launch officer, assigned to McConnell AFB, Kansas, was on leave and had traveled home to Richmond, Virginia for the holidays and could have been this caller.[41]

On May 2, 1981, Lt Cooke departed McConnell AFB on leave, flying first to St. Louis and then to Washington, DC. At Washington National Airport, he checked his luggage in a locker and, empty handed, hailed a taxicab, returning shortly to the airport. The cabdriver said that he had dropped his passenger at the Soviet Embassy, but that the passenger had returned quickly because the Embassy was closed. Cooke then took a bus from the airport to his home in Richmond. He had failed to report his contacts with Soviet officials in violation of AFR 205-57, <u>Reporting Espionage, Sabotage and Subversion</u>, and was confronted by AFOSI.[42]

Christopher Cooke was born on July 14, 1955, at Fort Lee, Virginia. His father was fatally shot when Cooke was a child, and as he grew older, Cooke developed a suspicion

Volunteers

that his father had been murdered by his grandfather. Over the years, his family provided Cooke with little information about his father or the circumstances surrounding the shooting. After his arrest, a psychological examination disclosed an adolescent identity crisis which centered around the lack of information, he received as a child, concerning his father.[43] Although he had a strong dislike for his stepfather, he was close to his mother.

Cooke graduated from Old Dominion University in May 1978 and later earned a master's degree from William and Mary College. His thesis, completed in 1979 (as well as a 1978 guest editorial in a newspaper), centered around nuclear weaponry.[44] He applied twice, although unsuccessfully, to join the CIA and was in the process of preparing a third application at the time of his arrest.[45] Although he was raised as a Catholic, he espoused a belief in Hinduism (nonpracticing) and traveled to Bombay, India, during the summer of 1979 to visit an Indian woman he had met and fallen in love with while at William and Mary College.[46]

On one occasion, his stepfather threw him out of the house when he came home one evening and expressed the view that socialism was better than capitalism.[47] He entered the USAF and was assigned to Medina AFB, Texas for Officer Training School. He was considered to be a "know it all," argumentative, intelligent, insecure, and not well-liked by his peers.[48]

After receiving a commission and completing missile launch officer training, he was granted a Top Secret security clearance and assigned to the 532 Strategic Missile Squadron at McConnell AFB. At the time of his arrest, he was 25 years old and unmarried. He had ordered a book from Walden Books in Witchita, Kansas entitled <u>Wilderness of Mirrors</u>, by David C. Martin, which had recently been published in paperback and concerned the CIA and counterintelligence matters. Cooke apparently was fascinated with espionage, constantly talking to his friends and coworkers, and even acting out some of his fantasies.[49]

When first interviewed, **Cooke** claimed to have a serious interest in political science and explained that his contacts with the Soviets were to ensure future employment with the U.S. Government. In effect, he hoped to make a name for himself as a great political scientist. Cooke claimed that his contacts with the Soviets were made to persuade them to let him publish "a breakthrough in Soviet foreign policy." He was vague when it came to explaining what this new "breakthrough" would be. He went on to describe various overt and quasi-secret attempts to engage the Soviets in this legitimate task--hoping to convince the Soviets that he could be discreet and trusted as a political analyst if they wanted to announce their change in foreign policy through him.

Although he had been rebuffed by the Soviets (not surprisingly), he remained keen on the idea that someday he would be able to persuade them to use him to announce a foreign policy breakthrough. According to **Cooke**, his first attempt to contact the Soviets was on June 15 or 16, 1980, from a hotel in St. Louis and again during June 24 to June 30 from his apartment in Witchita. During the second

Volunteers

telephone call, he offered to provide copies of Emergency War Orders, but was rebuffed. Cooke described these attempts as "spontaneous," although he noted that the "thought of committing espionage was ever present in my mind." When Cooke became Deputy Commander of his missile crew, he seriously began to think about selling information to the Soviets, but could not explain why.

In September, he borrowed a friend's Kodak 110 instamatic camera to photograph documents at the missile site, while a coworker slept. Cooke tried to develop the film in his apartment, but was unsuccessful. In late September or early October, he again attempted to photograph documents, but this time had the film developed at a local photo store, requesting that only negatives be made. He admitted providing these to Soviet officials in Washington, DC. He claimed that in late November or early December, he copied information onto computer paper which was located at the missile site. Cooke used his crew bag to carry the papers out of the missile area. He typed a note to the Soviets regarding his willingness to provide information concerning nuclear strike capabilities and added instructions for a personal meeting on December 19, 1980, at the Holiday Inn in Richmond, Virginia.

When he visited the Embassy on December 17, 1980, he left the note and classified materials with the receptionist inside the Soviet Embassy. The receptionist asked him to write his name on a small index card and he wrote "Mark Johnson." Underneath the name "Johnson" he wrote "Scorpion."

On December 19, 1980, he telephoned the Holiday Inn asking if "Sally Rogers" (a name he had specifically asked that the Soviets use for the woman he requested they send to the hotel to meet him)[*] had registered and became frustrated when he discovered she had not. Although confused and extremely frustrated by the Soviets' lack of interest, Cooke was undaunted in his desire to commit espionage.

On December 22, 1980, he telephoned the Embassy, using the name Johnson, and on December 23 drove his mother's car to Washington, but used a taxi to go to the Embassy after the car broke down. Cooke was paid $50 by the Soviets for handwritten notes he had copied from classified material. They allowed him to use the telephone to call home and tell his parents the car had broken down and that he would be late in returning. Cooke went back to Richmond and shortly after the holidays resumed duty at McConnell AFB.

From February to April 1981, Cooke continued to gather classified information from his duty section. In May, Cooke returned to Washington, DC and Richmond on leave. He expected the Soviets to telephone him on May 3, 1981, and when they did not, he telephoned them on May 4, again extremely frustrated at being rebuffed. Cooke claimed that money was not his motivation (although he was going to ask the Soviets for $3,000) but that he was trying to live out his fantasies of espionage.[50] He intended to ask them for

---

[*] A psychologist who later interviewed Cooke noted that he was "attracted to older foreign women." The psychologist also noted that Cooke was not by nature a criminal, spy, or ideologically pro-Soviet, but instead his actions were the result of internal emotional disorders.

111

Volunteers

1,000 British pounds ($2,000) and a British passport. If the Soviets had asked, Cooke was prepared to travel abroad to meet with them.

During an interview, Cooke requested legal counsel and a grant of immunity before being interviewed further. Legal officials were contacted and based on their advice, Cooke was given an oral agreement of immunity so that a damage assessment could be accomplished. Later he was charged with violation of Article 92, <u>Uniform Code of Military Justice</u>, for failing to obey a lawful order or regulation (AFR 205-57).

On February 22, 1982, the Court of Military Appeals issued a decision, in which the majority held that prosecution of Cooke constituted a violation of due process of law. This was based on the court's opinion that "de facto" immunity had been granted and that Cooke held a reasonable expectation that if he satisfactorily cooperated with USAF officials in their damage assessment, there would be no court-martial.

Crest[*]

On December 29, 1976, Sergeant Crest, a transportation specialist assigned to the 40th Tactical Fighter Group, Aviano AB, Italy, was stopped at the West German border by Bavarian police while attempting to enter the country from the German Democratic Republic (GDR). This was not an authorized border-crossing area for military personnel and the Bavarian police alerted U.S. military authorities. When

---
[*] pseudonym

apprehended and interviewed by military policemen from the U.S. Army, **Crest** admitted that he had been to West Berlin and did not realize he was traveling through the GDR as well as crossing the border at an unauthorized location. He was found to be in possession of 14 cartons of cigarettes and two USAF identification cards. The military police believed that he was involved in blackmarket activities and alerted AFOSI which assumed control of the investigation.[51]

AFOSI investigation and subsequent interviews with **Crest** disclosed that he had been born in Budapest, Hungary on June 15, 1949. His parents separated in 1951 and he lived with his grandmother until his parents divorced in 1953 or 1954. **Crest's** mother emigrated to the United States; however, he remained behind, with his grandmother. In 1963, he decided to join his mother; but, the Hungarian Government would not allow him to leave. **Crest** attempted suicide, and shortly afterward was reinterviewed by Hungarian officials and allowed to emigrate to the United States.

In 1966, **Crest** decided to return to Hungary, claiming a strong desire to see his father and because of acrimonious feelings towards his mother for deserting him when he was an infant. Upon arrival in Hungary, he was interrogated for 3 days by Hungarian internal security officers. He completed the equivalent of a high school education while in Hungary, and then worked as a chauffeur for a clothing firm in Budapest. In November 1967, he was drafted into the Hungarian Army as a truckdriver.[52]

Crest was discharged from the Hungarian Army in 1969 and married a woman from an upper-class family in Budapest. He worked as a chauffeur for the National Oil and Gas Trust Company. Although he later claimed not to have been a member of the Communist Party, his wife joined the Party despite his objections.[53] The National Oil and Gas Trust Company laid off personnel, including **Crest**. He claimed to have taken "sick leave" and "recuperated in a mental hospital for six months." He returned to work at the same company, again as a driver, but claimed to have become disillusioned and to have wanted to leave Hungary. **Crest** alleged that he was selected to be the chauffeur for the President of Hungary in May 1973, but turned the position down when he was told he had to join the Communist Party. **Crest** also stated that he had been interviewed to be a chauffeur for the Hungarian Intelligence Service (AVH).

In late 1973, he devised a plan to go on a honeymoon with his wife in West Germany and, once in the West, he intended to persuade her to seek political asylum with him instead of returning to Hungary. While in West Germany, he informed his wife of his plans, but she returned to Hungary claiming that she wanted to be with her parents who were ill. **Crest** remained in the West and, in September 1973, he arrived in New York to live with his mother.[54]

In November 1973, **Crest** enlisted in the USAF and was assigned to Aircraft Maintenance School, where he failed the training course. He remained on active duty, first assigned to a field maintenance squadron and later to the base motor pool. He claimed to have faked a hearing problem to have his job changed from the field maintenance squadron to the motor pool.[55] In May 1976, he was assigned to the base motor pool at Aviano AB, Italy. Soon after, he purchased a 1972 BMW sedan, paying $2,500 cash--a considerable sum of money to most junior enlisted personnel at that time.[56]

Upon his enlistment in the Air Force, **Crest** had failed to annotate on his Personal History Statement (DD Form 398) that he had served in the Hungarian Army, had traveled to various foreign countries, and that his former wife and mother were both members of the Communist Party.

Crest's mother, when interviewed, related that after her divorce she remarried and fled Hungary in 1956 during the revolution. She claimed that she was unable to bring her son with her, but had vowed to get him out of Hungary. In addition, she claimed that she paid a substantial sum of money to a high-ranking Hungarian official to have her son's travel visa approved.[57]

During the course of the investigation and several extensive interviews, **Crest** often contradicted previous statements or became vague on certain issues, leading investigators to believe that **Crest** was not only involved in blackmarketing, but also that he had failed to report contacts with Hungarian intelligence officials. Investigators considered **Crest** to be intelligent and adventuresome, but this did not fully account for his behavior.[58] **Crest** requested an exculpatory polygraph examination which was administered on February 8, 1977. The examiner noted that he was deceptive in his responses to questions concerning his involvement with a hostile intelligence service.

Volunteers

Crest's lawyer requested that another polygraph examination be administered because he felt that during the first examination, **Crest's** deceptive responses were the result of his not being truthful about his involvement in blackmarket activities. On March 8, 1978, a second polygraph examination was administered (after clarification of issues relating to his involvement in blackmarket activities). The following questions were asked during this examination:

> Were you knowingly providing material to a hostile intelligence service?
>
> Have you ever knowingly received anything from a non-U.S. intelligence service?
>
> Are you now working for a non-U.S. intelligence service?
>
> Since joining the USAF, have you purposely been in contact with a non-U.S. intelligence service?
>
> Since becoming a USAF member, have you received any payments from a non-U.S. intelligence service?
>
> While a member of the USAF, have you provided a non-U.S. intelligence service with any USAF material?

Crest's responses to these questions also indicated that he was deceptive concerning his involvement with a hostile intelligence service. No legal evidence was developed during the investigation, but he was administratively discharged from the USAF.

On 11 and 12 June 1986, **Crest** voluntarily contacted counterintelligence officials to make a statement concerning his case. Although he gave a lengthy description of his life in Hungary and his enlistment in the USAF, **Crest** continued to deny any involvement with a hostile intelligence service. This more recent statement not only contained several contradictions to previously made statements, but also appeared to be an attempt to rationalize his misfortune at having been detected because he made a careless mistake.

Crest told investigators that the reason he failed his polygraph examinations was that he had tried to deceive the examiner concerning his blackmarket activities. This may have been true on the first test; however, **Crest** conveniently forgot to mention to the interviewers that prior to his second polygraph examination the blackmarketing activities had been disclosed and clarified. Therefore, **Crest** knew the questions being asked during the examination would not pertain to blackmarketing.[59]

John Allen Davies

On October 27, 1986, the FBI arrested **John Allen Davies**, a 33-year-old San Jose, California resident, and formerly a Staff Sergeant in the USAF, and charged him with attempting to deliver classified U.S. military information to an undercover agent posing as a Soviet official during a meeting in San Francisco's Golden Gate Park. **Davies** was arrested at Ford Aerospace Communications Corporation in Palo

Volunteers

Alto, where he had been employed as a laboratory technician since leaving the USAF on June 11, 1984.[60]

An FBI affidavit, filed in U.S. District Court in San Francisco, indicated that **Davies** had contacted the Soviet Consulate in San Francisco and offered to provide information on USAF reconnaissance efforts. He was subsequently met by an undercover FBI agent posing as a Soviet official from the consulate.[61]

During his meeting with the undercover agent, **Davies** expressed willingness to turn classified information over to the Soviets "out of revenge because of the unfair way he was treated while in the USAF and that he also wanted to do something to embarrass the United States and interfere with the effectiveness of its reconnaissance activities."[62]

Davies was born on August 29, 1953, in England and was a U.S. naturalized citizen. He entered active duty on March 28, 1974, and was assigned to Shaw AFB, South Carolina; Kadena AB, Japan; Osan AB, Korea; and Lowry AFB, Colorado, before his assignment to Rhein-Main AB, Germany.

Davies was an Avionic Sensor System Specialist, with 10 years in the USAF when he was discharged in June 1984 for unsatisfactory duty performance. In 1975, he was apprehended by USAF Security Police while leaving an air base when a drug detection dog "alerted" on marijuana in his car. In a recent news interview after his arrest for espionage, **Davies** admitted to being a heavy drug and alcohol user.[63]

His final assignment was as a sensor repairman on C-130 aircraft assigned to the 7580th Operations Squadron, Rhein-Main AB, Germany.[64] **Davies** did not hold a security clearance or have access to classified information at Ford Aerospace Corporation and was arrested before being able to provide any information to the Soviet Union.[65] If he had not been arrested and had managed to sell the classified information to the Soviet Union, he would have disclosed sensitive operational data pertaining to Air Force electronic and avionic systems. **Davies** was tried and convicted, receiving a 5-year sentence.

Raymond George DeChamplain

On June 5, 1971, it was learned that Viktor Vladimir Mizan, a Third Secretary at the Soviet Embassy, and a known KGB officer in Bangkok, Thailand, was in contact with a U.S. serviceman for the purposes of committing espionage. The serviceman had been previously in contact with Yuri Markin (another known KGB officer who had recently returned to the Soviet Union) and was in contact with Mizen to provide him with information Markin had requested. Mizin was observed meeting with an individual who was later identified as MSgt **Raymond George DeChamplain**, a direct descendant of Samuel DeChamplain, the famous French explorer and founder of the Canadian province of Quebec.[66]

Surveillance coverage was initiated on **DeChamplain** and a second contact with the Soviets was observed which **DeChamplain** had failed to report as required by USAF

Volunteers

Regulations. On July 2, 1971, AFOSI detected **DeChamplain** removing a Top Secret document from his duty section, along with three Secret and several unclassified documents. **DeChamplain** was observed taking a taxi from his residence and heading for downtown Bangkok, and was apprehended as he was about to deliver the package of classified material to Mizan. At the time of his arrest, **DeChamplain** was 40 years old and had over 20 years in the Air Force.[67]

DeChamplain was born on August 6, 1931 in Hartford, Connecticut. He was raised in a white, lower middle-class neighborhood, along with his three sisters and two brothers. Without any civilian job prospects, he enlisted in the USAF in 1951 at the age of 19, after dropping out of the University of Maryland. His assignments included tours in Japan, France, Germany, and Italy before being assigned to Thailand in November 1967.

His first assignment was at U-tapao Air Base, approximately 140 kilometers from Bangkok. In June 1969, he was transferred to Don Muang Air Base, only 16 kilometers from Bangkok. This suited **DeChamplain's** present lifestyle. He enjoyed frequenting the many bars in Bangkok where military personnel spent their off-duty time, with his favorite bar being the Sea Hag, a known homosexual hangout.

He worked as an administrative specialist and at the time of his apprehension he was assigned as the Non-Commissioned Officer in Charge (NCOIC) of J-1 (personnel) at the Joint U.S. Military Advisory Group (JUSMAG) in Bangkok. His duty performance was poor and his coworkers describe him as inattentive, incompetent, and frequently absent from his duty station. He was disliked by his coworkers and often derided, although he tried hard to make friends by freely spending his money--even on those who mistreated him. Although not popular with his peers, he quickly acquired a good grasp of the Thai language (not an easy feat) and made several close friends within the Thai community. (DeChamplain's feelings of alienation are similar to those of Mira.) Although many coworkers knew of DeChamplain's homosexual relationships with young Thais, they did not report his activities to his commander. His coworkers and others who knew him described him as being "weak, vulnerable to persuasion, moody and a carouser."[68]

He was granted a Top Secret clearance in 1966. Eventually, he successfully completed a high school equivalency examination and accumulated 15 hours of college credit.

While in Thailand, DeChamplain married a Thai woman; however, after a few weeks she moved out. There is strong evidence which indicates that DeChamplain was having a homosexual relationship with his brother-in-law (a musician) who, after his sister moved out, continued to live with DeChamplain.

DeChamplain did not appear to have any strong political convictions; however, he was chronically in debt. His landlady, Mrs. Tipya Sirikul, said that DeChamplain rented a house from her and that he seemed poor compared with other GI's. He usually asked her if he could put off paying the rent for a few days.* DeChamplain admitted to investigators that he had always been bad at managing his money and frequently took out one loan to pay off another, resulting in a debt exceeding $13,000.

DeChamplain alleged that he had been blackmailed by the Soviets into committing espionage (Chapter 2), but this seems unlikely. Although a Soviet intelligence spotter seems to have introduced him to Markin at a party, Markin did not follow up on the introduction. It was DeChamplain who, 4 years later, approached the Soviets (after some prompting from the same spotter who instructed him to contact a GRU officer, who decided not to deal with DeChamplain and instead had him contact Mizin), and the evidence indicates he volunteered to betray his country in an effort to obtain money to repay some of his debts.[69]

DeChamplain had between five and ten personal meetings with the KGB in Thailand before being apprehended. DeChamplain was provided with a codename, verbal recognition codes (parole), and safety signals. Because he was bringing out such large quantities of documents, the KGB feared that their operation would be detected and they would lose a valuable volunteer that was successfully being exploited.

---

*Mrs. Sirikul claimed to have attended a party at DeChamplain's residence where some of the male guests wore women's clothing. When DeChamplain was arrested, Mrs. Sirikul believed it was for homosexuality (Bangkok Post, July 28, 1971).

In order to overcome this problem the KGB prepared to train him in the use of a camera, so that he could photograph the documents instead of removing them from the office. In July 1971, he was scheduled to receive training on the Minox camera and other methods of clandestine communication and operation, but was arrested beforehand.

Although he had only received $3,800, he had been promised additional payments ranging from between $10,000 and $25,000. He was also to be paid a retainer of $400 per month.

During the few days of his treason, **DeChamplain's** duty performance improved tremendously. He suddenly volunteered for extra work, taking over duties processing and distributing all Top Secret documents. All he had to do was to briefly delay in-processing the documents and he could then remove them to show the KGB, or copy them if necessary. The destruction of Top Secret documents requires that a witness be present, but **DeChamplain** falsified the necessary signatures. He came to work early and volunteered to stay late to keep up with his office work, but in reality, this provided him with uninterrupted access to the office copy machine. When questioned by investigators about which documents he passed to the KGB, **DeChamplain** nonchalantly pointed to all the safes in the room indicating that he passed everything to which he had access.

In November 1971, **DeChamplain** was convicted at a court-martial and sentenced to 15 years confinement, reduction to the lowest grade, and forfeiture of all pay and allowances. This sentence was later reduced to 7 years confinement at hard labor.[70]

Volunteers

George J. French

On April 5, 1957, an individual attempted to personally deliver a letter to the Soviet Embassy in Washington, DC, by placing the letter inside a newspaper and leaving it on the Embassy grounds. The newspaper was recovered by the FBI and was found to contain a note with information identifying a hotel room in New York City (room 1877, Hotel New Yorker); instructions on how to make contact with the individual; and an offer to commit espionage.[71] The note included an offer to sell "valuable military information," including diagrams of weapons for $27,500. A check of the hotel disclosed that Captain **George H. French**, from Mount Vernon, New York, and a bombardier-navigator assigned to the 60th Bombardment Squadron, Ramey AFB, Puerto Rico, was registered in the room described in the note to the Soviets.

AFOSI and FBI agents, posing as Soviet Intelligence officers, followed the instructions provided by **French** in the note and met him in his hotel room in New York City. Believing the AFOSI and FBI agents to be Soviet Intelligence, **French** offered to sell classified drawings, but indicated that they were in Puerto Rico. The agents identified themselves and arrested **French**.

A search of his room revealed a key to a train station locker and **French** led agents to the locker which contained classified notes and diagrams pertaining to special weapons

Figure 32

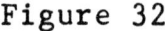

Captain George French

research and development. The sketches and notes concerned special weapons fuse and control systems, along with circuit wiring diagrams of the weapons. A search of his residence in Puerto Rico disclosed 60 classified documents which **French** had collected and intended to provide at a later date to Soviet intelligence officers.

French had served in both World War II and the Korean War, and had received several decorations during a distinguished career to include the American Defense Service Medal and the Air Medal with five oak leaf clusters. In Europe, he flew 35 combat missions as a B-17 bombardier and navigator, and during the Korean War he flew five combat missions in B-29's.[72]

His wife attributed her husband's espionage attempt to financial difficulties. He was supporting a family of 5 on $803.38 a month.[73] Captain **French** was addicted to gambling and could not afford the stakes he lost. His gambling losses apparently resulted in a debt of over $8,000 or almost 1 year of pay.[74]

On September 20, 1957, after a 5-month investigation, **French** pled guilty and was convicted of espionage at a court-martial. He received a life sentence; however, although the conviction was upheld, the sentence was reduced to 10 years.[75]

Case Summaries

Oliver Everett Grunden

In September 1973, an AFOSI source[76] reported that Airman First Class Oliver Grunden, a 20-year-old airman assigned to the 100th Organizational Maintenance Squadron, Davis Monthan AFB, Arizona, was attempting to sell classified information concerning the U-2 aircraft.[77] AFOSI's source informed Grunden that she might be able to introduce him to someone who would be willing to purchase the classified information.

Grunden provided the source with a tape recording containing classified information pertaining to U-2 tail numbers, performance data, overflight information, and Olympic Fire Missions. Later, Grunden met with two AFOSI special agents posing as Soviet intelligence officers[78] and was paid $950 for two sheets of paper which contained classified information concerning the U-2 aircraft. Grunden additionally offered to take the two "Soviet" intelligence officers on a tour of the base and flightline to observe the U-2 aircraft. Grunden was confronted and apprehended by AFOSI.

Grunden was born on July 27, 1953, in Mitchell, Indiana and raised in a white, middle-class family. After graduating from high school, he entered the USAF in 1973 at age 19, and after basic and technical training was assigned as a maintenance specialist for the U-2. Grunden had been granted a Secret security clearance.[79]

Volunteers

At the time of his attempted espionage, he was married, had one child, and his wife was pregnant with their second child; however, the couple had separated and his wife was living with her parents. He was described as being weak, naive, immature, and a carouser. His motivation for committing espionage was strictly financial gain.

In March 1974, **Grunden** was tried by court-martial and convicted, receiving a 5-year prison sentence, reduction in grade to Airman Basic, forfeiture of all pay and allowances in excess of $300 a month, and a dishonorable discharge. The U.S. Court of Military Appeals overturned his conviction based on prosecution procedural errors and, in March 1977, **Grunden** was re-tried and again found guilty, with his sentence reduced to time already served.

Herman*

During the mid-1960's, it was learned that the KGB had successfully recruited an espionage agent within USAF Intelligence in Europe in 1959. In May 1968, an AFOSI investigation identified Master Sergeant **Herman** as the probable suspect. Further investigation continued, until July 1970, in an effort to establish a clandestine espionage relationship (and evidence) between **Herman** and the KGB. When he was finally confronted by counterintelligence investigators, he denied any involvement in espionage, making no admissions, nor providing any information which

---

*pseudonym

could have been used as evidence or to assess the damage he may have caused. He was polygraphed on two occasions and was considered by the examiner to be deceptive both times regarding key questions concerning his involvement in espionage with the KGB.[80]

Herman was born on July 17, 1927 in Romania (in a area which is now part of Hungary). His parents were Romanian Jews and he started attending Hebrew school at age 3. He attended Romanian public schools from 1934 until the Jews were banned from them in 1939. He worked as an apprentice printer with his uncle until 1944, when the Jews were forced to live in the Jewish ghetto by the Nazis. Three weeks later he and his family were sent to the Auschwitz concentration camp, where his parents, six brothers, and several other family members were murdered by the Nazis. He was transferred to various other camps until he was liberated by the Soviet Army in 1945, when he was 17 years old.

According to **Herman**, in September 1945, he returned to Romania and then in November he traveled to Fuerth, West Germany where he remained until 1949. On February 2, 1949, he entered the United States in New York City under the Displaced Persons Act and he worked in a bakery while attending night school to learn English. Because of his poor job prospects, he enlisted in the USAF on August 10, 1949, at age 22, and was assigned as a cook. In April 1951, he was assigned as a language technician to the 1133rd Special Activities Squadron at Ft. Myer, Virginia, and later was assigned to Vienna, Austria; Ent AFB, Colorado; Bolling AFB,

Washington, DC; and in August 1955, Rhein Main AB, West Germany. During this period he completed the high school equivalency examination and began work on a college degree.

After his tour of duty at Rhein Main, he was assigned to Munich, Nurenburg, Bad Soden, and then the Defector Refugee Center in Frankfurt where he worked as an interrogator. While assigned to Frankfurt, he had also traveled to Yugoslavia on a short, temporary duty assignment.

In July 1959, he was assigned to Webb AFB, Texas, as a finance clerk, but he returned to the Defector Refugee Center in June 1962 and remained there until April 1966, when he was assigned to Vandenburg AFB, California, until November 1967, as a finance clerk.

In 1967, he received an Associate of Arts Degree. He was fluent in Hungarian, Romanian, Spanish, Hebrew, German, and English. In May 1968 (after attending the Area Intelligence Course at Ft. Holabird, Maryland), he was assigned to the Special Activities Group at Camp King, Oberusel, West Germany.[81]

His coworkers described him as being extremely intelligent and his Airman Performance Reports were always above average. His wife was German and vehemently anti-American, never trying to acquire U.S. citizenship. **Herman** was extremely religious and followed strict Jewish practices. He was considered by many coworkers to be moralistic and idealistic, extremely antiofficer and antiauthoritarian. Several of his superiors considered him to be weak, dull, moody, and cunning.

Because he made no admissions following his arrest, it is difficult to determine the exact reasons for his involvement in espionage. He may have had some pro-Soviet feelings as a result of his liberation from the German concentration camp; however, financial gain was likely another factor. Additionally, it must be remembered that **Herman** grew up in what British author Andrew Boyle refers to as "the climate of treason." This refers to the period when Soviet intelligence was able to recruit many ideological traitors such as Philby, Burgess, Blunt, Fuchs, Gold, McClean, Greenglass, and the Rosenburgs, among many others. **Herman's** case was administratively adjudicated and he was honorably retired with over 30 years service in the USAF.[82]

John P. Jones

On September 21, 1952, AFOSI apprehended Staff Sergeant John P. **Jones**, assigned to the Headquarters Squadron, Taegu, Korea and a resident of Manchester, Massachusetts, for conspiring to "give intelligence to the enemy." Apprehended along with **Jones** was Staff Sergeant Giuseppe E. Cascio.

Jones provided classified information to Cascio, which Cascio in turn provided to a Korean national. Cascio was tried and convicted, receiving a 20-year prison sentence. **Jones** was not charged and returned to the United States after a medical board declared him to be insane and incompetent to stand trial.[83]

Volunteers

Joseph Patrick Kauffman

Joseph P. **Kauffman** was born on August 10, 1918 in Rutland, Vermont, a small, New England farming village. His parents were born in Russia, (his father was from St. Petersburg, now called Leningrad) emigrated to England and Canada, and, in 1913, settled in Vermont. **Kauffman's** mother died when he was 4 years old and his father died shortly afterwards. His two brothers, and a sister were shuffled through 15 sets of foster parents, and basically raised in a series of lower, middle-class environments. In 1946, his sister, who was working towards her doctorate degree, committed suicide. One brother went on to become a Major General in the U.S. Army Reserves and a senior executive with Sears and Roebuck. His other brother (Charles)[*] was an interior decorator. Relations with his older brother were remote and casual, but not unfriendly. On the other hand, **Kauffman** had deep affection and admiration for his brother Charles, who was the executor and beneficiary of his will. Charles was active in the U.S. Communist Party and a dedicated Marxist; he fought with the Abraham Lincoln Brigade on the Loyalist side during the Spanish Civil War from 1936 to 1938.[84]

---

[*] When he became a Marxist, Charles legally changed his name to Keith.

Case Summaries

During World War II, **Kauffman** was an administrative assistant to a flight surgeon while serving in Africa and Arabia. He later attended Officer Training School for medical-administrative personnel and was commissioned in 1945. In 1946, he left the service and went to work for the U.S. Department of Agriculture in New York City, where he lived with his brother Charles for several months.

Kauffman earned a Bachelor of Science degree in Agriculture. In April 1951, he was recalled to active duty and entered the USAF as a finance officer. He was quickly promoted and earned a Bronze Star. From June to September 1956, **Kauffman** was hospitalized for a psychiatric disorder. According to hospital reports, he had a compulsion to correct all kinds of deficiencies. He was described by coworkers as being unproductive, going through the desks of personnel at night, and behaving and speaking in a vulgar and offensive manner. According to one diagnosis, he "appeared to be adjusting on an obsessive-compulsive level, apparently in defense of some underlying paranoid feelings." The report indicated, however, that he generally controlled his feelings and there was no indication of any active, significant psychiatric disorder.

Kauffman felt his education and experience should have resulted in more responsibilities and recognition, but, instead, he had been passed over for promotion. His disgruntlement could have been a motivating factor in committing espionage.[85]

Volunteers

Coworkers described him as possessing above-average intelligence, having an interest in reading poetry, and being knowledgeable about classical music and the arts. He was also known to hike, fish, and participate in gymnastics. However, he was considered to be emotionally weak, effeminate, and used frequent obscene gestures and profanity in the presence of coworkers, supervisors, and subordinates.[*]

Kauffman was obsessed with the sanitization in the rest rooms and work areas. In addition, he was described as being high-strung, nervous, excitable, abrasive, and crude. Although he was known to have had heterosexual romances, there were also unsubstantiated allegations that he was a homosexual. He was extremely friendly with a known homosexual living in Baltimore and was alleged to have been involved in several other homosexual incidents.[**] Several who knew him noted that he was obsessed with financial matters, had a compulsive desire to accumulate wealth, and

---

[*] These were believed to be defensive mechanisms. (Interview with Brigadier General Richard S. Beyea, Jr.)

[**] Shortly after being assigned to Castle AFB, Kauffman was arrested for being drunk and disorderly outside a tavern in Atwater, California. The arresting officer thought that Kauffman had "designs" on two or three 16-year-old youths who fled when the police arrived. At Castle AFB, there were also unproven allegations that Kauffman had sex with several young airmen assigned to the base. During his interviews with AFOSI concerning his involvement in espionage, it was the accusations concerning homosexuality which concerned Kauffman the most, not his espionage.

was considered to be a miser. He was not well liked and had no real close friends. Kauffman was "anti-establishment," frequently causing difficulties with his superiors by not following their instructions.

After completing a tour of assignment in Greenland, Kauffman traveled to Europe on vacation before being reassigned to Castle AFB, California. It was during this vacation in Europe that he became involved in espionage.[86]

In June 1961, Karl Maennel Guenter, a First Lieutenant in the East German intelligence and security apparatus, defected to the West. Maennel identified Kauffman as an espionage agent whom he had personally interviewed and recruited. According to Maennel, who testified at Kauffman's trial,[*] Kauffman came to his attention on September 29, 1960, after he had been arrested by East German police for riding on an unauthorized train. Shortly after interviewing Kauffman, Maennel stated that he had been ordered out of the room by Colonel Yevgeniy A. Zaostrovstev, a Soviet Intelligence officer, who had served in Washington, DC as Second Secretary at the Soviet Embassy from August 1957 to May 1959.

According to Maennel, Zaostrovstev was asked to quietly leave the United States because of his espionage activities. In August 1960, Zaostrovstev was assigned to the Soviet Embassy in East Berlin undercover as Cultural Attache and Second Secretary. Zaostrovstev's primary objective was to

---

[*]Maennel would later testify at the trial of Harold N. Borger.

Volunteers

develop and recruit U.S. military and civilian employees in West Berlin.[87]

Maennel notes that Zaostrovstev interrogated **Kauffman** for about 1-1/2 hours. They initially had a heated argument which Maennel believed was the result of **Kauffman** not liking Zaostrovstev. According to Maennel, **Kauffman** gave the interrogators an estimate of personnel strength; the type and number of aircraft; missions; and morale of personnel assigned to Sondrestrom AB, Greenland, and similar information about bases in Japan, where **Kauffman** had previously been assigned.

On September 30, 1960, **Kauffman** signed a statement to the effect that he had entered East Germany without proper authorization and had been treated well by East German authorities. Maennel noted that, because he was cooperative, **Kauffman** was instructed to stay in a hotel in West Berlin and return to East Berlin the following day for additional discussions.

During this initial contact with **Kauffman**, the East Germans were strongly convinced that he would return the next day as scheduled and indeed, **Kauffman** willingly returned to East Berlin. East German intelligence officers, including Maennel, took **Kauffman** out for a night on the town. **Kauffman** returned to West Berlin that night and, on the following day, he went back to East Berlin for a tour of the city provided by Maennel and other East German intelligence officials.

During this tour, while visiting Hitler's wartime bunker, **Kauffman** hid behind Maennel to avoid being seen by a U.S. Army captain in uniform who was on an authorized tour. At the end of the day, **Kauffman** agreed to return the following day. The next day, **Kauffman** was taken to a safehouse where he was provided with instructions for remaining in contact when he returned to the United States. **Kauffman** claimed that he did not have access to any sensitive information, but Maennel explained that was not a problem because seemingly unimportant information could be useful to them.

Specifically, **Kauffman** was asked to provide information concerning his fellow officers. He agreed to furnish biographic information, particularly weaknesses and vices, of officers he met. **Kauffman** told Maennel that he was a career officer, but did not like the way the services were run and stated that many Americans were sympathetic to communism. Maennel wrote the name and address of Klara Weiss in **Kauffman**'s notebook (an accommodation address) so that **Kauffman** could remain in touch.

Kauffman was instructed not to send reports to the address; he was to type his letters in English and begin with the salutation "Dear Aunt." The contents did not matter and he was to sign the letter with a different name each time he wrote. In addition, he was given a codename for identification purposes.

He was instructed to collect information and return to East Germany in 1963 to make his report, receive further instructions, and tradecraft training. The East Germans

Volunteers

advised **Kauffman** that they would pay for his travel and for the information he provided. When they presented **Kauffman** with a written agreement, he refused to sign, but indicated a willingness to work for them and asked if a handshake would be acceptable. Maennel stated that **Kauffman** was sympathetic to communism, but that money was his true motivation. Maennel believed that the Soviets eventually took over **Kauffman**'s case from the East Germans.[88]

After his initial contacts with hostile intelligence officers in East Germany, **Kauffman** finished his vacation in Europe and reported to his new duty assignment, the 93rd Combat Support Squadron at Castle AFB, California, where he worked in the Comptroller Office. Shortly after his arrival at Castle, but prior to his arrest for being drunk and disorderly, **Kauffman** had an emotional session with his supervisor and threatened to commit suicide if his career was jeopardized by an unfavorable Officer Effectiveness Report.

Kauffman, at age 44 was unmarried, had 15 years of military service, and had recently been passed over for promotion to Major. Before the Soviets could contact **Kauffman** after taking over the case from the EGIS, Maennel defected and **Kauffman** was apprehended by AFOSI. At the trial, **Kauffman**'s defense lawyer argued that **Kauffman** had been pressured into committing espionage and that the entire incident was a big misunderstanding. The prosecution noted, however, that **Kauffman** not only traveled in East Germany on an unauthorized train, but that he had made the reservations on September 23 for travel on September 29, obviously not a last-minute decision. Maennel's testimony (noting that **Kauffman** "had been easy to recruit" and willingly returned to East Berlin on several occasions) persuaded the jury. **Kauffman** was convicted by court-martial and sentenced to 20 years confinement, although, on appeal his sentence was reduced to 2 years.[89]

Francisco De Asis Mira

On March 24, 1983, a USAF member telephoned AFOSI at Bitburg AB, West Germany, stating that a friend had a problem involving a security matter. The caller advised that his friend had been solicited for defense information. Because of the sensitivity of the conversation, the call was quickly terminated after AFOSI agents made arrangements to meet with the caller and his friend on the following day.[90] On March 25, 1983, AFOSI interviewed the USAF member and it was determined that he had no personal knowledge of the incident. He introduced his friend, Sergeant **Francisco De Asis Mira**, a coworker assigned to Detachment 1, 601 Tactical Control Group, Birkenfeld, West Germany.[91]

Mira was born on January 18, 1960, in Spain, and his father was the Spanish Military Attache at the Spanish Embassy in Ottawa, Canada. **Mira** was a 23-year-old unmarried computer technican who had joined the USAF in 1979. Prior to his assignment to Birkenfeld, **Mira** had been stationed at Lackland, Keesler, and Luke USAF AFB's.[92] He was interviewed and claimed to have lived in 1982 with a West

Volunteers

German woman whom he suspected of being involved with the Red Army Faction, a Marxist-Leninist-oriented terrorist group operating in West Germany.

About the same time, his girlfriend introduced him to Helge Stoeppke (born: December 25, 1957) and Ralf Dietmar Antes (born: May 26, 1956), two West German nationals who were involved in drug activities and armed robberies. **Mira** claimed that Stoeppke and Antes started asking questions about his job in the USAF. **Mira** alleged that he had reported his suspicions to AFOSI at Ramstein AB, Germany, and believed AFOSI either was uninterested or needed more evidence. **Mira** stated that he decided to develop additional information by himself. He claimed that his subsequent contacts with Antes and Stoeppke were designed to develop additional information.[93]*

According to **Mira**, Antes and Stoeppke began asking more specific questions concerning his duties and informed him

---

*This "defense" is not unusual. **Mueller**, and other captured traitors have rationalized their espionage and betrayal as working as a "double-agent." To be a double-agent, the person must be working under the control and direction of two different intelligence services, for example the United States and the Soviet Union, with the Soviets believing that they have recruited a legitimate spy and the United States allowing them to believe that this is the case. With **Mira**, **Mueller**, and others using this defense, they betrayed their country, and did not come to the attention of U.S. counterintelligence until they were caught. They did not contact the intelligence service on behalf of U.S. counterintelligence and therefore cannot be considered a "double-agent."

that they had a contact in East Berlin who would be willing to pay for information. He claimed that he removed a classified North Atlantic Treaty Organization (NATO) document from his duty section and showed the cover sheet to Stoeppke and Antes. At this point, AFOSI stopped **Mira's** interview and advised him of his rights for unauthorized removal of a classified document.

Mira declined legal counsel and continued his story. He then explained that, in order to gather evidence that Antes and Stoeppke were involved in espionage, he showed them cover sheets of classified documents so as to establish credibility. He claimed that Antes and Stoeppke visited East Berlin in December 1982 and were rebuffed by the KGB, but later, in January 1983, the Soviets contacted them and asked them to return to East Berlin. **Mira** alleged that Stoeppke and Antes returned from this trip to East Berlin with 7,000DM (exchange rate of 2.6 DM: 1 U.S. dollar) and gave him 2,400DM. The Soviets also provided instructions for **Mira** to purchase a camera and for Stoeppke and Antes to have future meetings in East Berlin with the KGB. **Mira** claimed that he realized he was "in over his head" and that was why he had contacted AFOSI.[94]

AFOSI agents, not believing **Mira's** story, assisted him in preparing his statement and requested that he take a polygraph examination. While the statement was being typed and **Mira** was waiting for his polygraph examination, he began to display signs of apprehension. Eventually, **Mira** admitted that much of the information he had provided AFOSI

Volunteers

had been inaccurate and he wanted to clarify his original statement.

In subsequent interviews **Mira** admitted to having provided 3-1/2 rolls of film containing classified information to Antes and Stoeppke, who in turn passed the film to the Soviets in East Berlin. **Mira** also admitted that he had originated the idea to commit espionage to make some money and then enlisted Antes and Stoeppke to assist him.

Mira took photographs[*] of classified codebooks, maintenance schedules, and status boards for Antes and Stoeppke to sell in East Berlin. The Germans made five trips to East Berlin in late 1982 and early 1983. On the first trip, they asked an East German border guard if they could speak with a KGB officer because they had important information. They were introduced to a man who paid them DM7,000 and they gave **Mira** DM2,400 when they returned. **Mira** gave DM2,000 to his girlfriend to deposit in her bank account. Antes and Stoeppke were given an emergency telephone number in Leipzig, East Germany in the event that they had to contact their case officer prior to the next scheduled meeting.[95]

According to Stoeppke, **Mira** made a request (through Stoeppke) to Soviet Intelligence for an electronic device to open a safe at Birkenfeld and a smaller camera to use in photographing documents in the safe. **Mira** apparently

---

[*]**Mira** used a camera in his office at night to photograph documents. He developed his film at the base photo hobby shop. **Mira** also removed documents marked for destruction.

believed the safe contained information of high classification. The Soviets refused the request, but provided money for the camera and asked for photographs of the three men to be used on false British passports.[96]

Mira may have believed (correctly) that Antes and Stoeppke were "ripping him off" and he wanted to get even with them, while extricating himself from his predicament. He developed the idea to report, through an unwitting coworker, that he had been approached and solicited for information by a hostile intelligence service.

Mira's motivation was also based on financial gain; however, this was coupled with his desire to become part of the "in" crowd. Mira was not well liked by his coworkers, nor did he like them. He felt more comfortable with the German "in" crowd, and Antes and Stoeppke appeared to be the most popular. Although Mira was a fringe member of this "in" crowd, he needed more attention and devised the idea to commit espionage. Not only would this make money quicker than drug dealing, but Mira would become the center of attention with Antes, Stoeppke, and his girlfriend. It was only when he realized that he was being used that Mira sought to extricate himself from a bad situation and he approached AFOSI not realizing how thorough the investigative process would be. Once he realized that his story was only getting him in deeper, he quickly faced reality and confessed.

Antes and Stoeppke were arrested by West German authorities and confessed, implicating Mira. Antes and Stoeppke were convicted in German Federal Court, each

Volunteers

receiving a 3-1/2-year prison sentence. **Mira** was convicted by a court-martial, receiving a dishonorable discharge and a 10-year prison sentence; however, a pre-trial sentence agreement of 7 years in prison, which had been arranged by **Mira's** defense lawyer in return for a guilty plea, was imposed.

Gustav Adolph Mueller

On October 26, 1949, Corporal Gustav Adolph **Mueller**, a 19-year-old student assigned to the European Command Intelligence School in Oberammergau, Germany, was apprehended by U.S. counterintelligence agents posing as Soviet Intelligence officials when **Mueller** attempted to provide them with two classified documents. Another student assigned to the intelligence school became suspicious of a telegram **Mueller** sent, under an assumed name, to the Soviet Embassy in Bern, Switzerland, and notified counterintelligence authorities. The student advised that he was with **Mueller** at the Garmisch Recreation Center when the message to the Soviets was sent. In the message, **Mueller** asked to make contact with Soviet representatives and signed the message with the name John S. Watson. Counterintelligence officials, posing as Soviet Intelligence officers, contacted **Mueller** as he requested in his telegram.[97]

Mueller, the son of an English mother and Swiss father, was born in Rangoon, Burma. He was raised there until his father was murdered by Japanese soldiers invading Burma. In addition, **Mueller** claimed that his two sisters died on Burma Road, fleeing from invading Japanese forces. He and his mother then went to Calcutta, India, and they eventually emigrated to the United States. His mother remarried, and settled in St. Paul, Minnesota. **Mueller** enlisted in the USAF in 1947, after attending the University of Minnesota for 1 year. According to the student who reported **Mueller** to counterintelligence authorities, **Mueller** claimed that his father fought with Lenin in 1917 for the liberation of Russia and **Mueller** appeared to be a Communist sympathizer.[98]

Counterintelligence agents arranged to meet with **Mueller** in a hotel room in Garmisch. He went there believing he would be meeting with Soviet representatives. While one "Soviet" talked with **Mueller**, three other counterintelligence officers took turns listening at the keyhole of the door. According to agents testifying at the trial, **Mueller** told the "Soviet," "It is easy to steal U.S. secret documents,* Americans are so careless." **Mueller** claimed he was not motivated by money, only his idealism.[99]

On April 15, 1950, **Mueller** was convicted of attempting to deliver U.S. secrets to Soviet officials and was sentenced to 5 years in prison and a dishonorable discharge. He was likely the first serviceman since World War II to have tried to betray military information to the Soviet Union. **Mueller** claimed that he was concerned about Communism at

---

*Mueller claimed to have slipped the classified documents out of a folder in the school library, when the librarian was not looking.

the Oberammergau Intelligence School and had sent the message to Bern in an effort to lure Soviet officials to Germany to entrap them.* "I thought I would play along with them and win their confidence. Then when I had proof enough against them, I would tell my commanding officer."

Mueller denied being a Communist or sympathetic to Communism. He later admitted that he had sent the telegram on "a juvenile impulse."[100] Mueller was described as being immature and his actions seem to support this opinion. Adventure, fantasy, immaturity, and thrill appear to be at the center of his motivation to commit espionage.

Bruce Damian Ott

In early January 1986, the FBI advised AFOSI that Sergeant **Bruce D. Ott**, assigned to the 1st Strategic Reconnaissance Wing, Beale AFB, California, had contacted Soviet officials at the Soviet Consulate in San Francisco and offered to commit espionage. On January 11, 1986, Ott was contacted by an official of the Soviet Consulate (in actuality an FBI agent posing as the Soviet official) to arrange for a meeting as Ott requested.[101]

Two days later, Ott told the "Soviet" official that he had access to classified defense information concerning the SR-71 aircraft which he would like to sell to the Soviet

---

*This defense is not uncommon. Thirty-three years after **Mueller's** trial in Germany, **Mira** made the same claim at his trial in Germany.

Union. Ott also told the "Soviet" official that he would like to be a "long-term mole" and arrange his career so that he could have a long-term association with the Soviets.* He provided the "Soviet" official with a copy of the 1st Strategic Reconnaissance Squadron recall roster (which was marked For Official Use Only) and a handwritten list of the types of classified documents to which he had access and would try to obtain.

On January 20, 1986, Ott again contacted Soviet officials at the Soviet Consulate in San Francisco. The FBI agent, posing as a "Soviet" official then contacted Ott, who stated that he needed $600 immediately and that he could not obtain any information until he had the money.[102]

Ott was contacted by the "Soviet" official on January 21, 1986, and Ott again stated that he needed $600 in order to get his car back (it had been repossessed). Later, the "Soviet" official paid him $600 for which Ott signed a receipt using a pseudonym. Ott agreed to bring classified information to a meeting on the next day.

Indeed, Ott provided a copy of Strategic Air Command (SAC) Regulation 55-2, Volume XI, entitled <u>SAC Tactical Doctrine for SR-71 Aircrews</u>, dated July 16, 1982, which was the most current version of this regulation and classified Secret. Ott allowed the regulation to be photographed and agreed to obtain additional classified information in the

---

*A "mole" in espionage parlance is an agent who has infiltrated his way into an organization without being detected.

Volunteers

future. The "Soviet" official paid Ott $400.[103] Ott was then apprehended by AFOSI Special Agents, and made several spontaneous comments such as:[104]

> Thanks for catching me before this got out of hand.
>
> You caught me red handed--I will provide a statement after speaking with my lawyer.
>
> Oh I really screwed up.
>
> I'm going to be a model prisoner. How much time do you think I'll get?

Investigation by AFOSI disclosed that during the period Ott was attempting to commit espionage, he was also busy planning how he was going to invest his money. He discussed buying three houses (one for him, one for a friend, and another for rental income) with real estate agents, and he planned to buy a new car, paying $16,000 in cash. The story he related was that he would soon have $165,000[105] (Ott had demanded $165,000 to be paid in three installments by the "Soviet" official) from the sale of his accounting business (which did not exist). Ott was in serious financial difficulties and his motivation to commit espionage was to extricate himself from debt. Ott was described by several friends as being immature, quiet, naive, and friendly. At the time of his apprehension, he had recently (January 2, 1986) checked out from the base library a book entitled The

New KGB. His attempt at espionage came after several months of almost daily television and news stories concerning espionage and defections.

Ott was born in Erie, Pennsylvania[106] on March 11, 1960, and raised by his parents in a white, middle-class family environment. He was the oldest of three children but was not close to his father. Throughout high school, Ott was a conscientious student and graduated in the upper third of his class with nearly a B average. Although he was described as "studious" by several high school acquaintances, he was also considered to be "high strung" and sometimes difficult to get along with. After finishing high school, Ott joined the Army Reserves. Supervisors and coworkers described him as always attempting to excel and suffering from an inferiority complex. They generally agreed that he was loud and boisterous at work, immature, and having a difficult time handling pressure, in addition to having poor leadership qualities. After serving in the Army Reserves from December 1978 to January 1984, Ott enlisted in the USAF on January 9, 1984 and was assigned as an administrative clerk for the 1st Strategic Reconnaissance Squadron, Beale AFB, California. He met and married a local woman shortly before his arrest for espionage. Ott told his new wife and her family that he was better off than he really was; however, his future in-laws did not believe him.[107]

When Ott was 15 or 16 years old, he began working as an altar boy in the local Catholic church.[108] His priest admitted that he performed fellatio on Ott (several times the first year, but gradually decreasing in frequency until there was no sexual contact) while Ott was working in the church. The priest stated that Ott was not a homosexual because he did not reciprocate the fellatio. The priest also said that in 1979 or 1980, Ott returned home on leave from the Army and met with him at his residence, where he performed fellatio on Ott.

Ott was described by a psychologist who tested him after his apprehension as "independent in his thinking" and having an IQ of 108 (estimate based on the Shipley Institute of Living Scale). The psychologist noted that Ott had "difficulty with high-order cognitive processes, specifically in the area of logic" and was "passive and unassertive." Ott told the psychologist, "My father and I were never that close." He also indicated that he had a difficult time growing up as a child. One agent, who apprehended and later interviewed Ott, described him as being a loner, usually quiet, but capable of displaying fits of anger. He described Ott as a hard worker, but ineffectual, having a tendency to brag and "put on airs."[109]

On August 6, 1986, Ott was convicted at a general court-martial for failing to report unauthorized contacts, attempting to deliver a classified document to a foreign agent, and for unauthorized removal of classified information from his duty section. He was sentenced to serve 25 years at hard labor.[110] According to Ott's defense lawyer, Ott was a "damaged individual who desperately turned to a spy attempt as a release from pressures and to save his fading self-image."[111]

Case Summaries

Walter T. Perkins

On October 18, 1971, MSgt **Walter T. Perkins**, a 36-year-old intelligence specialist at the Air Defense Weapons Center, Tyndal AFB, Florida, was apprehended at the airport in Panama City, Florida, by AFOSI as he started to board a flight to Mexico City.[112] In his briefcase, **Perkins** carried one USAF and four Defense Intelligence Agency (DIA) classified documents totaling 600 pages.[113] Also in his possession were operational instructions for meeting his hostile case officer in Mexico City, Mexico.

On the following day, after being alerted by U.S. authorities, the Mexican Federal Security Service detained Oleg A. Shevchenko, a GRU officer working undercover at the Soviet Embassy in Mexico City, who was waiting for **Perkins** at the prearranged meet location. Mexican authorities released Shevchenko and expelled him from the country.[114]

Volunteers

Perkins was born on February 8, 1935 in Perry, New York and was raised in a lower middle-class neighborhood. He managed to graduate from high school, with a "D" scholastic average, apparently more as a result of attitude than intelligence, as he later completed almost 2 years at the University of Maryland and was considered to be intelligent and shrewd by many of his coworkers.[115] Upon completion of high school, **Perkins** had several jobs during a short civilian career. He worked in a cannery, as a gardener, and as a handyman at a restaurant but was dismissed after 3 weeks for being unreliable.

With no future job prospects at age 17, **Perkins** joined the USAF at Parks AFB, California on December 1, 1952, and spent his entire career working in various intelligence-related assignments, including stints in radio traffic analysis, operations, and support. The Airman Performance Reports **Perkins** received reflect that he was intelligent and competent. He developed only a few good friends with no real, long-lasting relationships. He was described as opinionated, moody, and inflexible. **Perkins** developed the habit of submitting destruction certificates to coworkers who certified the destroying of material which they did not witness. When **Perkins** was assigned in Japan, six secret aerial photographs were discovered to be missing which could not be explained. **Perkins** later denied that he had provided these documents to the Soviets, although in hindsight, he appears to be the logical suspect.[116]

During his first assignment in Japan, **Perkins** met a local bar girl, with whom he would live with for the remainder of his tour. Eventually he received orders reassigning him to Turkey and told the Japanese bar girl that he would marry her when he returned to Japan. When **Perkins** was reassigned to Japan, he kept his word and married the former bar girl. His wife had a difficult time learning English, understanding American culture, and adjusting to military life. **Perkins** was extremely reluctant to take his wife out with him and she thought he was ashamed of her. Outwardly she was devoted to him, professed to love him, and catered to his every whim and need in the traditional Japanese manner. Eventually, his wife overcame many of her problems and learned to speak and read English.

Her improvement apparently had little effect on **Perkins**. By this time he had established quite a reputation as a heavy drinker (his wife would later testify that he drank a fifth of whiskey every day) and a carouser. Although he was not generally considered to be handsome, he perceived himself to be a "lady-killer." **Perkins** did most of his socializing with barmaids and low-class women. He had numerous extra-marital affairs and all of them appear to have been with Oriental women. Although **Perkins** was raised as a Catholic, there is no indication that he was faithful to the church or its teachings. His wife resented his drinking and carousing, especially when he stayed out all night and returned home only to dress for work. **Perkins** remained sober in the office, but nearly every night after work he visited the NCO club to drink and gamble. After the club closed, he went to a bar or his home to continue drinking. At his trial, **Perkins'** defense lawyer argued that he was an alcoholic. **Perkins** was generally a good father to his children, although at his trial his wife testified that he did occasionally beat the children. Investigators learned of many rumors or "hints" that **Perkins** was a homosexual, but no specific or substantiated information was ever developed.[117]

Through technical and human source coverage, AFOSI discovered that **Perkins** was removing classified documents (he possessed a Top Secret - Special Intelligence clearance) from his duty section and was planning to travel to Mexico City. To this point, the investigation had disclosed that **Perkins** had previously made two trips to Mexico City. AFOSI decided to apprehend **Perkins** at the Panama City Airport once it was confirmed that he was leaving the country with the classified documents.

During initial interviews, he refused to disclose how he had become involved in espionage activities. He stated that while working in intelligence he had read several AFOSI <u>Counterintelligence Special Studies</u> concerning espionage agents and describing their motivations and backgrounds. **Perkins** was embarrassed and did not want his life story described in a USAF report.

In later interviews, **Perkins** provided some details, but often his information could not be verified through either investigative actions or polygraph examinations. Finally, a short time after he had been released from prison, **Perkins** gave some details, but, again, often his information could not be verified. He stated that he had not received any money, except reimbursement for travel expenses. **Perkins** claimed that he was approached by the Soviets in Japan and shown a picture of a young Vietnamese child. The Soviets told **Perkins** they had located his Vietnamese girlfriend and their child and would not harm them if **Perkins** cooperated with the Soviets. Although there is little evidence to substantiate this story, it is probably the most accurate account of his initial recruitment by the Soviets.[118]

Perkins initially may have been blackmailed into committing espionage, but evidence suggests that not only was he paid above and beyond his expenses, his lifestyle may have made it plainly obvious to the Soviets that he could be approached and recruited with little effort on their part. At the time **Perkins** became involved in espionage, Soviet intelligence officers were quite open and blatant in their approaches to servicemen stationed in Japan. KGB and GRU officers were known to "troll" the bars searching for potential espionage agents. **Perkins** showed obvious signs of affluence: buying new and expensive clothes and furniture, investing in a bar in Japan, and paying cash for a new car. During the course of the espionage operation, **Perkins** suggested ways to improve operational security or take the initiative to keep in contact with the Soviets. The initial approach and recruitment of **Perkins** may have been conducted by the Soviets based on blackmail, but it appears that once involved, **Perkins** became "hooked" on the financial aspects and thrill of being involved in a clandestine operation.

Perkins had personal meetings with GRU officers in New York, Japan, Mexico City, and New Orleans. He was also given an accommodation address in Miami, which he claimed to have used on two occasions, but without success. **Perkins** used a briefcase to remove documents from his duty section; however, prior to his assignment to the Air Defense Weapons Center at Tyndall, he microfilmed the documents he provided to the Soviets. He denied providing the Soviets with Top Secret, Special Intelligence, or Strategic Integrated Operations Plan (SIOP) material while assigned to Tyndall AFB. He usually passed the actual document to the Soviets because it had been certified as being destroyed. Although **Perkins** claimed that he was neither provided with additional tradecraft training, nor used it, he was suspected of receiving one-way-voice-link (OWVL) messages on a short-wave radio which was found during a search of his home by counterintelligence personnel.[119]

Perkins claimed to have provided the GRU in Japan with 11 or 12 DIA documents between December 1968 and January 1969 which were secret intelligence assessments on the People's Republic of China and North Korea. He also claimed to have passed an SAC document concerning Soviet Air Defense Systems, but denied this in subsequent interviews. **Perkins** was 34 years old at the time he became involved with the Soviets and felt that his abilities were not being fully utilized.[120] **Perkins** was convicted and received a sentence of 3 years confinement; reduction to Airman Basic; a dishonorable discharge; and forfeiture of $150 a month for 36 months.[121]

Robert Glenn Thompson

On June 7, 1963, an FBI surveillance team observed a personal meeting in Lynnbrook, New York, between Fedor D. Kudashkin, a known KGB officer, and an individual subsequently identified as Robert Glenn **Thompson**, a former USAF member who had been discharged in 1962 and was at the time driving a fuel delivery truck. The investigation continued until January 1965 when **Thompson** was arrested by the FBI.[122]

According to records, **Thompson** was born on January 20, 1935, in Detroit, Michigan, one of two children, and raised by Episcopalian parents in a lower middle-class neighborhood. Information developed during the course of the investigation and **Thompson's** imprisonment indicates that he was born on January 23, 1925 in Leipsig, Germany, the son of a German father and Russian mother. He joined a Nazi Youth Brigade and was captured by the Soviet Army in 1945. It appears **Thompson** was brought into the Soviet intelligence apparatus (in prison **Thompson** claimed he was a KGB major) and trained as an "illegal." Illegals are specially trained individuals, sometimes an intelligence officer and other times not, who is given a false identity (legend) and enters the targeted country with documents supporting the legend. Illegals are controlled directly from their home country and report directly to their intelligence service headquarters. Rarely, if ever, would an illegal have contact with the legal intelligence officer working under cover as a diplomat, journalist, or trade official. On one occasion, **Thompson** is known to have assisted another Soviet illegal across the Canadian border and may have been the support officer for an illegals network operating in the United States. His job as a truckdriver provided excellent cover because it allowed him to come and go as he pleased.

When **Thompson** was 6 years old, his father died. Although he stuttered, high school tests reflected that he had above-average intelligence and reading ability; however, he continually was absent from class and therefore received low grades. As an adult, tests showed that he possessed below-average to average intelligence. His attitude towards school was described as "apathetic."[123] He dropped out of high school with a "D" average, while in the 10th grade. **Thompson** held several manual jobs, but had few prospects; therefore, he enlisted in the USAF in December 1972, at age 17. He later claimed that he enlisted in order to avoid being drafted.[124]

After completing basic military training, **Thompson** was assigned to aircraft engine mechanic technical training, but a back injury resulted in a transfer to administrative duties. Eventually he was assigned to the Air Force Office of Special Investigations in Berlin, as an administrative clerk. **Thompson** was constantly bragging and showing off, wanting to be a "big-wheel." Coworkers described him as weak, anti-officer, and a malcontent who drank excessively.

He was frequently moody and envious of the Special Agents assigned to his office. **Thompson** suffered from a skin disorder and pockmarks and was extremely sensitive about his appearance. A loud and boisterous carouser, he had no close friends, was suspected of being unfaithful to his German wife, and was not particularly devoted to his children. When his wife moved to the United States in February 1957, **Thompson** is suspected to have lived with another woman.[125]

He was reprimanded by his Commanding Officer for reporting to work unshaven and unkempt and was later reduced in grade from Airman First Class to Airman Second Class by a court-martial for leaving his place of duty; intoxication while on duty; and wrongful appropriation of a .38 caliber revolver. **Thompson** exhibited a number of personal weaknesses which could easily have attracted the attention of a hostile intelligence service, especially considering his access to classified information.[126] One unusual characteristic was his obsession with the color red. **Thompson** wore red clothes, dressed his children in red clothes, painted his house and fuel truck red, and when arrested claimed that he detected surveillance because of a small red light which kept flashing off and on inside a car which he believed to be the red light on a radio which lights up during a transmission.

Although **Thompson** gave three accounts of how he became involved in espionage (Chapter 2), there is little doubt that he volunteered, either because he needed money and was disgruntled with his status in life or because of ties

Volunteers

established at the end of the war when he was captured by the Soviet Army.

Thompson was quickly indoctrinated into espionage tradecraft. He was given a Minox camera and provided with instruction in its use. He was also given a shoe with a concealment device located in the heel. The heel twisted off to reveal a compartment which could then be used to hide two rolls of film.[127] Thompson claimed that he was also given four electric outlets which were actually microphones, to screw in office walls.[128] He said that the Soviets flew him to the Soviet Union in December 1957 for additional training. Also, Thompson stated that his training included the use of secret writing carbon and that he was given an address book in which the last two pages contained such carbons. He was taught how to receive messages on a shortwave radio and advised to listen for broadcasts on Thursdays at 0705 hours. Thompson also stated that he was instructed in microphotography. When his training was completed, he was given $1,000 to purchase a shortwave radio and a 35mm reflex camera.[129] Thompson received more than $4,000 for services to the KGB.

According to Thompson, his training officer in the Soviet Union was an attractive woman who later met him in the United States at his first personal meeting with the KGB since his reassignment to Malmstrom AFB, Montana.[130] Thompson had arranged the meeting by sending a letter in secret writing to his accommodation address in East Germany. In December 1958, he was honorably discharged from the USAF and thought he would not be of any further use to the KGB. However, the KGB instructed him to rejoin any branch of the service, the FBI, or AFOSI, and gave him $300.[131] He was tasked to gather background information concerning a police officer in Detroit, Michigan, and asked to obtain information or photographs of missile bases in Michigan. After moving to Long Island, New York, he was sent to Canada to find Igor Gouzenko, a Soviet intelligence code clerk who defected in 1946, and to photograph power plants and stations on Long Island, FBI offices, and FBI vehicles.[132]

Thompson provided the KGB with information concerning AFOSI counterintelligence activities in Berlin; personality data on Special Agents; safe house locations; positive intelligence activity and information; deployment of KC-97 aircraft from Malmstrom AFB, Montana; shipment of missiles and jet fighters from Detroit; and industrial information from Detroit and Long Island.[133] **Thompson** was prosecuted and pled guilty, receiving a 30-year sentence. In 1978, he was traded to East Germany in exchange for Israeli pilot, Miran Marcus, age 24, who was being held in Mozambique. **Thompson's** exchange was highly unusual as far as the Soviets are concerned. Generally they will abandon traitors and only attempt to have their own citizens and intelligence officers returned. This adds credence to the evidence indicating that **Thompson** was an illegal.[134]

Volunteers

Walton*

During the late 1960's, it was learned that a black American man, approximately 30 years old, was involved in espionage activities on behalf of the GRU. An extensive espionage investigation lasted almost 6 years, but was closed after all logical investigative leads had been pursued and the suspect had not been identified. The investigation was reopened when it was learned that the unidentified traitor was a former U.S. Army soldier who had been assigned to Germany in 1964, prior to his enlistment in the USAF. The unidentified suspect was eventually identified as **Walton** and he was located in Houston, Texas, working as a cabdriver.[135]

Walton was born in Houston, Texas, on November 16, 1939. His civilian job prospects were not promising, so **Walton** entered the U.S. Army on October 27, 1961. He was discharged on October 26, 1964. Several months later, he enlisted in the USAF. **Walton** received a bachelor of science degree in sociology from Parkhill College in Mississippi and also attended a university in Germany, after his discharge from the Army in order to learn the German language.

Walton was separated from the USAF on August 18, 1972, after submitting a request for discharge. He felt that he had been discriminated against because he had not been promoted or selected to attend Officer Training School. In both his Army and USAF careers, **Walton** was a personnel specialist.[136]

---

*pseudonym

Walton was granted immunity from prosecution by the Department of Justice in return for a full account of his espionage activities. The details of Walton's involvement in espionage remain classified.

Wesson*

Normally, those who commit espionage go to extreme lengths to ensure that they are never detected. The case of Wesson is unique in that he came forward and admitted he had committed espionage on behalf of Soviet Intelligence while on active duty with the USAF. However, Wesson did not make this startling disclosure until he had been arrested by police for being involved in a bank fraud scheme, but there is little doubt that his story is true.[137]

Wesson was born in Birkenhead, Cheshire, England on September 6, 1934, and Wesson was raised by his mother (a Methodist) in a white, lower-class neighborhood. After graduating from high school, he made $18 a week as an office boy. Wesson served in the USAF from March 22, 1957 until July 1963 as an airborne radio operator. He was assigned to Landstuhl AB, Ramstein AB, and Tempelhof AB, Germany, before his assignment to Castle AFB, California. While assigned to Castle, Wesson changed his job from that of an airborne radio operator to a defensive fire control system operator. While in the USAF, Wesson married a German woman

---

*pseudonym

Volunteers

Walton was separated from the USAF on August 18, 1972, after submitting a request for discharge. He felt that he had been discriminated against because he had not been promoted or selected to attend Officer Training School. In both his Army and USAF careers, **Walton** was a personnel specialist.[138]

Walton was granted immunity from prosecution by the Department of Justice in return for a full account of his espionage activities. The details of **Walton's** involvement in espionage remain classified.

James David Wood

James **Wood** (also known as James David Gilmore) was born on June 28, 1938, in Tacoma, Washington, the second child in a lower, middle-class, white Protestant family. His father, died when **Wood** was 4 years old. After graduating from Fife High School, **Wood** worked as a clerk at the Boeing Aircraft Company, and attended the University of Washington as an engineering student, and when 20 years old, he enlisted in the USAF on May 8, 1958, serving as an intelligence specialist in technical collection systems.*

Wood learned to speak Russian at the Defense Language Institute in late 1958, and was an Honor Graduate from

---

*Wood enlisted in the USAF after pneumonia and a lack of money prevented him from continuing college after his high school scholarships had run out.[139]

Syracuse University where he completed an intermediate Russian language course in 1963. He later completed a Czechoslovakian language course there, graduating at the top of his class.

Wood applied for duty as a Special Agent with AFOSI because of the low promotion opportunities in his career field and he was worried that his sons would be embarrassed because of his rank. His Airman Performance Reports were consistently outstanding and he was soon assigned to duties with AFOSI. Wood was articulate, imaginative, outgoing, outspoken, self-confident (if not arrogant), and dressed fashionably. He had been denied a commission because of a minor visual defect and was convinced that his rank was not adequate for a person of his intelligence and abilities. Politically, he was considered to be a liberal.[140]

On July 21, 1973, at 1805 hours, FBI surveillance observed Viktor Aleksandrovich Chernyshev[141] (a known KGB officer who was working undercover as the First Secretary at the Soviet Embassy in Washington, DC) enter a telephone booth in Queens, New York. A few moments later, an unidentified individual entered the adjoining telephone booth. Chernyshev left his booth and started walking along the street. The unidentified individual in the adjoining booth followed him and, after walking 2 blocks, Chernyshev turned and faced

Volunteers

the unidentified person.* FBI agents immediately detained Chernyshev and the other individual. Chernyshev, who was scheduled to return to the Soviet Union within the next few weeks, was released shortly after being detained. The unknown person was identified as James **Wood** and in his possession was a map which directed him to go to a nearby laundromat on the corners of 207th St. and Hillside Avenue in Queens. With the map was a note indicating that **Wood** had received $1,000 for information which he had previously provided. He also had several index cards which contained classified information concerning AFOSI counterespionage operations and instructions for a clandestine rendezvous with the KGB.[142]

Wood, a Technical Sergeant on the promotion list to Master Sergeant, was in New York enroute from Travis AFB, California to a new assignment at Ankara, Turkey. **Wood**'s wife and two children were in a nearby Ramada Inn, resting after a long day of sightseeing in Manhattan. A search of the area revealed a rental vehicle belonging to **Wood** and in its trunk there was a plastic garbage bag which contained 363 documents, approximately one-half classified either Confidential or Secret and the remainder marked For Official

---

*The Soviets had provided **Wood** with a parole (recognition phrase), but **Wood** and Chernyshev were detained by the FBI before the parole was used. According to **Wood**, the KGB officer was to say "Tell me please how can I get to the Belmot Race Track?" **Wood** was to respond with "I think you should go to Manhattan."

Use Only. The bulk of these were AFOSI reports and related correspondence; several were DOD and FBI reports.[143]

Under questioning, **Wood** related that he had developed the idea to commit espionage some time before his arrest. He took no positive action until March 1973, but had stockpiled classified documents. **Wood** said that this must have been an unconscious action.

In April 1973, **Wood** mailed a letter to the Soviet Consulate in San Francisco stating that he had access to sensitive information and, if the Soviets were interested, they should run an ad in a specific newspaper as a signal prior to leaving information for future meet instructions at a dead drop designated by **Wood** in his letter. The Soviets placed the advertisement and left instructions for **Wood** in the dead drop which he had selected. **Wood** was given the option of three places for meeting with the Soviets: New York, Montreal, or Mexico City. He was also given $1,000 and was instructed to make a red chalk mark (number 1, 2, or 3) representing New York, Montreal, or Mexico City on a specific bench in Aquatic Park, San Francisco, and place a personal notice* in a newspaper to alert the Soviets as to which meet location he had chosen. **Wood** chose New York because he would soon be traveling there on his way to a new assignment in Turkey.[144]

---

* The newspaper ad was to say "Alex D., please call Sally immediately when you are back from . . . (The city he chose was to be the end of the sentence.)

Volunteers

Wood, after 18 years in the USAF (3 years in AFOSI), claimed to have become dissatisfied with a system in which he could not get promoted. He considered his abilities and performance to be equal to or better than most commissioned officers and developed an antiofficer attitude. This may have been an underlying reason for Wood's attempt at espionage, but financial motivation was primary. Wood considered himself to be a "ladies man" and allegedly had several extra-marital affairs. He developed a weakness for women and alcoholic beverages, as well as gambling and losing frequently. Soon his financial obligations exceeded his lifestyle, leading him to seek out a method of obtaining additional money.

Wood admitted that it was financial difficulties on the part of his immediate family which led him to commit espionage, but that greed and the excitement of being involved in clandestine activity, as well as attempting to seek female companionship, soon became strong factors.[145] Wood had not been in contact with the KGB for very long before he was detected and, therefore, his actions caused minor damage. He may have sent some information of minor importance to establish his bona fides, but was apprehended at his first meeting with the Soviets. Wood pled guilty and received a dishonorable discharge and 7 years confinement, later reduced to 2 years because of his cooperation.[146]

Chapter 6

CONCLUSIONS

"They lack all loyalty and all guilt; they enjoy living on the edges and particularly need the excitement, the constant danger and adventure in order to carry on their lives."

**Conrad Hassel,
former FBI Special Agent**

In this study, the nature of espionage in the USAF has been examined in an effort to determine if there are any commonalities or characteristics among USAF espionage agents which could be exploited by security and counterintelligence officials to detect and prevent betrayal of our national defense secrets. Although much can be learned by comparing previous espionage cases, analyzing them for patterns and trends, and closely examining the sociological-psychological and environmental characteristics of USAF traitors, we cannot develop a set of "indicators" or a guide which can be used to determine who might become involved in espionage. Traditionally, the "indicators" of possible espionage involvement have included:

1. Foreign influence
2. Unexplained affluence
3. Financial difficulties
4. Disaffection
5. Questionable loyalty to the United States
6. Exploitable weaknesses or character defects
7. Excessive indulgence in alcohol or drugs

Volunteers

In addition to the above, the following factors were examined:
1. Educational status
2. Career field
3. Marital status
4. Age
5. Motivation
6. How espionage was initiated
7. Years of Federal service
8. Clandestine communications
9. Monetary payments
10. Traumatic childhood

As noted in this study, any USAF military member or civilian employee, regardless of career field, access to classified information, educational or social status, years of Federal service, age, race, sex, or assignment, could become involved in espionage and betray his or her country. This study, to some degree, supports the validity of the traditional investigative indicators and illustrates the many commonalities which exist among known USAF traitors, but it also illustrates that there are no absolute common denominators which are characteristic of all traitors which could be used to "profile" potential spies.

No two people are exactly alike; everyone has different experiences in life and reacts to situations based upon those experiences. Some individuals can cope with their character weaknesses or adverse situations which arise, while others cannot. Treason is both a criminal offense and an antisocial act, and no one can predict when a person will commit espionage in lieu of some other crime. In most cases, the USAF traitor appeared to be an opportunist--taking advantage of his or her access to classified information and providing it to someone he or she knew would pay large sums of money for it.

Conclusion

Obviously, because any USAF employee could become involved in espionage, Air Force officials, security managers, and counterintelligence specialists must remain constantly vigilant to the threat posed by hostile intelligence services and implement aggressive programs to neutralize the threat. Defensive security awareness and briefing programs alone are not the answer. In an open society with little historical sense of patriotism, and which glorifies treachery in books, television, and movies, an aggressive counterintelligence program will always be needed to ensure the security of our nation. Americans have often demonstrated their lack of historical perspective and have often championed the acts of individuals against society. For example, the film <u>Falcon and the Snowman</u> tends to glorify and empathize with the traitors, Boyce and Lee. Numerous other examples could be cited, but as illustrated in this study, most traitors, in reality, are extremely embarrassed by their treachery.

Defensive programs must be coupled with proactive counterespionage investigative programs, techniques, and offensive counterespionage operations. To most officials, "counterintelligence" implies "defensive" programs or actions. In reality, counterintelligence is much more effective at detecting and preventing espionage if it is "offensive" or proactive in its methods and techniques. Offensive utilization of human sources, defectors, technical and physical surveillance, and in-place defectors have provided the majority of espionage leads concerning USAF traitors and continued emphasis is needed if counterintelligence is to be successful in preventing treason.

Espionage in the USAF is not a problem which can be easily solved, nor is it ever likely to disappear. Counterespionage programs, in response to the real threat posed by foreign intelligence services, have always been and will continue to be both expensive and essential for our security. Although the Soviet Union and Warsaw Pact allies continue to pose the most serious espionage threat, other countries at times have also engaged in espionage against the United States and will continue to exploit opportunities in the future.

Money invested in developing and modernizing weapon systems, war plans, or secure communication networks is wasted every time a USAF member approaches a hostile intelligence service or is recruited to commit espionage. If these acts of betrayal cannot be prevented by defensive briefing and awareness programs, then the capability must exist to quickly detect and investigate acts of espionage, so that vulnerabilities to our defense can be corrected before exploited by our enemies.

Finally, it must be noted that detection and prevention of treason by itself cannot be the answer. Public awareness of the threat posed by foreign intelligence services can improve upon our security. Additionally, prosecution of traitors is also extremely important to the overall success of preventing espionage. Many years ago, most government agencies were reluctant to prosecute or publicize espionage cases. In some cases, the traitor was not prosecuted in order to to prevent the disclosure of sensitive sources and

Conclusion

techniques. Since the late 1970's, the United States has vigorously prosecuted cases of espionage. With each case, government officials must weigh two conflicting factors: the importance of prosecution and the damage a trial may pose to national security. As can be seen in Appendix 2, successful prosecutions can be achieved with little or no compromise of sensitive information.

Appendix 1[*]

HOSTILE INTELLIGENCE THREAT

SOURCES OF THE THREAT

-- <u>Overview</u>

Among foreign intelligence services, the Soviet services, the KGB, and the GRU,[**] represent by far the most significant intelligence threat. The Soviet threat is both the largest and, in terms of the ability and intent of the Soviets to act against U.S. interests, the most important. In fact, the activities of the Warsaw Pact and Cuban intelligence services are primarily significant to the degree that they support the objectives of the Soviets. The threat from intelligence activities by the People's Republic of China (PRC) is one of a different character. The first arrest of an American citizen on charges of committing espionage for the PRC occurred in 1985. Intelligence activities of another group of Marxist-Leninist states--Nicaragua, North Korea, and

---

[*]The following appendix is verbatim from an unclassified letter to Senator David Durenberger, Chairman, Select Committee on Intelligence, and from William J. Casey, Director of Central Intelligence, 29 Jul 86.

[**]The KGB, or Committee of State Security, and the GRU, the Chief Directorate for Intelligence, both operate on a worldwide basis. The KGB maintains internal security in the USSR and, as a secret intelligence service, conducts intelligence collection abroad, as well as covert political influence activities (active measures). The GRU as the military intelligence organization engages only in foreign intelligence.

Appendix 1

Vietnam--pose a lesser, but still significant, threat to U.S. foreign policy interests, although these countries have a limited official presence in the United States.

Many other countries--hostile, allied, friendly, and neutral--engage in intelligence operations against the United States. While these activities cannot be ignored, they do not represent a comparable threat. Nonetheless, in 1985, arrests for espionage included U.S. Government employees who were charged with passing classified information to Israel and who had disclosed the identities of CIA personnel and assets in Ghana.

-- <u>Soviet Union, Other Warsaw Pact, and Cuba</u>

The highest Soviet collection priority is accorded to policy and actions associated with U.S. strategic nuclear forces. Other high-priority subjects are key foreign policy matters, Congressional intentions, defense information, advanced dual-use technology, and U.S. intelligence sources and methods. The Soviets also target NATO intensively, partly as a means to obtain U.S. foreign policy and military information. The Soviets heavily influence the collection activity of the Cuban and Warsaw Pact services, in effect expanding their collection resources through exploitation of ethnic ties and the normally less-stringent U.S. controls on the activity of non-Soviets.

An open U.S. society permits the Soviets to acquire much of the information they require through nonclandestine means. Collection is carried out through diplomatic facilities, trade organizations, visitors, students, and

Volunteers

other open inquiry. It is aided by Soviet access to computerized U.S. and other Western reference systems, by U.S. Government programs designed to facilitate the legitimate dissemination of information, and by the U.S. Government's inability to exercise stringent controls over foreign visitors and exports.

The spearhead of the Soviet, other Warsaw Pact, and Cuban intelligence collection efforts is their official presence in the United States. In 1985, there were about 4,250 diplomats, commercial officials, and other representatives from Communist countries in the United States, 2,100 of whom are from the Soviet Union and other Warsaw Pact countries. Cuban and other Communist country officials are affiliated with their country's intelligence services. The Soviet Mission to the United Nations in New York has approximately 275 accredited diplomats; the Department of State has recently mandated a reduction in this number to 170 by April 1988.

The Soviet Union is using effectively United Nation (UN) organizations, particularly the Secretariat, in the conduct of its foreign relations and as a cover for the activities of Soviet intelligence service officers and co-optees. The UN employs, worldwide, approximately 800 Soviet nationals as international civil servants, with about 300 of them in New York. Approximately one-fourth of the Soviets in the Secretariat in New York are considered to be intelligence officers, and others are co-optees. Other Soviets in the Secretariat have been tasked to respond to KGB and GRU requests for assistance. The Soviet intelligence services

Appendix 1

also use activities; to spot, assess, and recruit American and foreign national agents; to support worldwide intelligence operations; and to collect scientific and technical information on the United States.

The KGB has succeeded in infiltrating its officers into the UN bureaucracy, with some reaching positions of authority. Also the KGB has held the position of Assistant to the Secretary General since Viktor Lesiovskiy held the post under U Thant. Currently, the Assistant is a KGB China expert. The Soviets take full advantage of UN personnel procedures such as liberal sick leave. This permits KGB UN employees to be absent as often as they desire, enabling them to carry out intelligence activities further abetted by the comparative freedom of movement enjoyed by UN employees.

Within the Soviet services, GRU personnel are targeted primarily against both military and scientific and technical information while KGB personnel are assigned to one of four operational departments or "lines"--Scientific and Technical (X), Political (PR), Counterintelligence (KR), or Illegals Support (N). S&T personnel specifically target U.S. advanced technology. Often, clandestine collection of S&T information is preferred over buying or developing technology because it is cheaper and provides the best short-term results, although there is a risk factor in the theft. KGB Line PR personnel target governmental policy information and, frequently, seek to advance Soviet objectives via contacts with persons of influence or through covert activities. Line KR officers have the security responsibility for preventing defections of Soviet personnel and particular concern for penetration of the U.S. Intelligence Community, although all lines are

Volunteers

tasked with this important function as a matter of general concern. Illegal support personnel comprise a small group involved with the operation of illegals--intelligence officers and agents infiltrated into the United States under false circumstances to operate clandestinely, having no overt connection with the Soviet Union.

The Soviets aggressively seek information on Western technology to avoid technological surprise and to improve their economy and weapons systems. Indications are that their acquisition efforts are becoming more selective than in the past, and that future collection will concentrate on technology which is used either in developing and producing U.S. weapons and military support equipment or which is specifically needed in Soviet industry for USSR weapons systems. The methods used to acquire technology will depend largely on the cost and the risk involved. It is likely that increased controls on trade with the Soviets and on Soviet visitors and official personnel will cause more changes in Soviet collection techniques. Even greater use of Warsaw Pact services as collectors, for example, is probable. More use of clandestine methods to acquire technology is also likely, when it cannot be obtained in other ways.

The extent of the hostile intelligence threat in the United States is further illustrated by the fact that the intelligence services of the USSR, other Warsaw Pact countries, and Cuba have about 130 diplomatic, commercial, and other entities in the United States which can be used as a cover for clandestine collection activities. The commercial presence of the Soviet Union and other Communist

Appendix 1

countries in the United States has been shown to afford their intelligence collectors wide opportunities. These commercial establishments (such as the USSR's Amtorg, and Intourist; the Polish Polamco; and similar East German, Czechoslovak, and other East European entities), through their legitimate activities, have access to Americans in business, industry, and government who are potential targets for agent recruitment. Economic data and advanced technology are the primary interests of the hostile collectors operating under commercial cover.

In addition to the threat posed by their official establishments, these intelligence services have infiltrated intelligence collectors into the United States among the thousands of exchange students, commercial and cultural visitors, tourists, and ship crewmen who enter this country each year. Further, in recent years, a number of intelligence agents of the USSR, Cuba, and other countries have been uncovered among the flood of immigrants into the United States from Communist countries. While not all of these agents are considered classic illegals, investigations have determined that many have been sent with intelligence missions. The deep-cover illegals, who are dispatched to the United States in the emigre flow and through other means by the Communist intelligence services, represent a particularly perplexing problem because of their completely clandestine manner of operation.

Volunteers

-- <u>People's Republic of China (PRC)</u>

The PRC has several intelligence services whose personnel are represented among the approximately 1,500 Chinese diplomats and commercial communities located at some 70 PRC establishments and offices in the United States. They also have some access to the approximately 15,000 Chinese students and 10,000 individuals arriving in 2,700 delegations each year. There is, of course, a large ethnic Chinese community.

Implications of the intelligence activities of the PRC are markedly different from those of the Soviet Union and its surrogates. The forces of the Warsaw Pact are arrayed against those of NATO; and the Soviet Union's expansionist policy poses a current and continuing global challenge to the United States and its allies. The PRC is not now in strategic competition with the United States. Indeed, the United States has fundamental interests in maintaining friendly relations with the PRC and in promoting its modernization, to include selective upgrade of its military defense capabilities. Collection priorities of the two major Communist powers reflect their respective foreign policies: the Soviet services with urgent requirements with respect to U.S. plans, intentions, and capabilities, as well as technology; the PRC services concentrated primarily on advance technology not subject to release to further PRC modernization in the 1990's and beyond. There is evidence that the PRC's traditional, careful, and patient development of assets has resulted in the establishment of a large human intelligence infrastructure in the United States.

Appendix 1

-- <u>Other Countries' Threats</u>

Other countries conduct human intelligence collection in the United States, both overt and clandestine. Their targets include the same range of interests as those of the Soviets, et al, including high technology and political, military, and economic policies and intentions which might impact in an adverse manner on the particular country.

Among the more common activities of foreign intelligence services in this country are attempts to penetrate emigre communities. A large number of expatriate political and ethnic groups in the United States are viewed as a threat by authorities in their former homelands. The list includes Libyans, Croatians, and Iranians, to name only some. From a national security viewpoint, these activities are of less significance than those of the USSR and its allies, although they are clearly in violation of U.S. sovereignty and may have an effect on U.S. foreign policy. Foreign intelligence services also target ethnic groups in the United States, directly or through front organizations, to influence U.S. decisions on foreign aid, trade agreements, and other issues in which the foreign government has valid interests.

HUMAN TARGETS

-- <u>Espionage</u>

During 1985, a total of 11 people were arrested and accused of spying for either the Soviet Union, its allies, or

Volunteers

other countries. Ten of them have since been convicted or pleaded guilty to espionage charges. Also, 11 persons who had been arrested on espionage charges during 1984 were subsequently convicted. Between 1 January 1981 and 31 December 1984, 23 arrests were made; from 1 January 1976 to 31 December 1980, 11 people were arrested; between 1 January 1966 and 31 December 1975, there were six espionage arrests. The spy of the 1980's has been described as a new breed, motivated more by greed than by ideology. However, the cases uncovered in 1985 demonstrate that this is not always the case--political beliefs, intrigue, job dissatisfaction, and alienation also appear to have been reasons for engaging in espionage. Moreover, 9 of the 11 noted above volunteered their services to the other side.

While in the past most espionage cases in the United States have involved the Soviet Union or other Warsaw Pact countries, in 1985 three arrests were markedly different. One was the first arrest of an American on charges of spying for the PRC. Larry Wu-Tai Chin, a retired CIA foreign media analyst, was charged and convicted of spying for the Chinese. He was a "plant" who received intelligence training before his employment by the U.S. Army in 1943. In a second case, charges of espionage were made against Sharon Marie Scranage, a CIA clerk who furnished a Ghanian national the names of CIA employees and assets in Ghana. Scranage was subsequently convicted. In the third case, Jonathan Jay Pollard, a civilian intelligence analyst with the Naval Investigative Service, pleaded guilty to criminal charges that he had illegally passed classified documents to Israel.

Appendix 1

The case involving John Anthony Walker, Jr., his son, Michael Lance, and his brother, Arthur James, was long-running and caused significant damage to U.S. national security. Walker admitted to having spied since 1968, and his information may have enabled the Soviets to read some of the U.S. Navy's most secret messages to the fleet, from the 1960's to the time of his arrest. His espionage activities have possibly reduced the U.S. lead in antisubmarine warfare. The three Walkers and a close friend, Jerry Alfred Whitworth, have been convicted for espionage.

Ronald William Pelton, a former NSA communications specialist from 1965 to 1979, was convicted of selling the Soviets information about a highly classified U.S. intelligence collection project targeted at the Soviet Union. Edward Howard, a former CIA officer, is accused of selling intelligence sercrets to the Soviets based on his knowledge of CIA operations in the Soviet Union. Howard, who resigned from CIA in 1983, disappeared from his home in New Mexico in September 1985.

Soviet intelligence efforts also include active programs outside the United States against U.S. Government personnel and businessmen. Even those recruited agents who live in the United States are frequently met in third countries to avoid U.S. domestic counterintelligence. KGB residencies emphasize that the principal targets are American Embassy employees, particularly code clerks and other communications personnel with access to classified information. Other targets include U.S. journalists, businessmen, and scientists who can furnish sensitive technology information, and students with job

Volunteers

prospects in sensitive positions for long-range development. Of concern are reported instructions from KGB Headquarters to its residencies that the KGB connection of some Soviet Embassy officers is to be made known so that a U.S. official considering volunteering his services would be aware of the right person to contact.

U.S. military installations and personnel abroad continue to attract major Soviet intelligence interest, both to gain potential access to military plans and to acquire sensitive technical data. There have been some recent instances in which the Soviets have contacted and attempted to recruit military personnel who have discussed financial or other personal problems during long-distance telephone calls to the United States from their overseas posts.

The widespread use of foreign nationals in U.S. Embassies and consulates compounds the problems faced by U.S. intelligence in most hostile countries. Over 9,800 foreign nationals are so employed for a number of reasons, including cost considerations. Despite their value in dealing with local government organizations because of their language fluency and understanding of local customs and regulations, the threat to U.S. security has been recognized. Even when barred from restricted areas in the official U.S. establishment, foreign nationals can glean information useful to the hostile security service, such as personal data on pay, movements, assignments, telephone calls, and vulnerabilities to recruitment.

The employment of foreign nationals in U.S. establishments in the Soviet Union and other Eastern European

Appendix 1

countries, as well as in numerous other countries where the Soviet Bloc has influence, affords hostile security services the opportunity to conduct a variety of technical penetrations. Offices, residences, and cars are all vulnerable to the planting of audio devices by foreign nationals with access, legitimate or otherwise, to the U.S. target.

Although all high technical threat posts have eliminated the access of foreign nationals from the vicinity of classified work areas, there remains a serious problem of common walls with uncontrolled adjacent areas from which technical attacks can be mounted. Offices and residences are also vulnerable to planted devices when access by foreign nationals is not properly monitored and routine technical countermeasures are not employed.

The U.S. Embassy in Moscow poses particular problems. Soviet nationals operate the carpool, including making mechanical repairs; staff the canteen where Embassy personnel gather for food and conversation; and until recently, operated the telephones. Approximately 200 Soviets are employed at the Embassy, contrasted to fewer than a dozen Americans in the Soviet establishments in Washington.

Soviet intelligence continues to successfully target foreign nationals employed by U.S. establishments abroad. The foreign nationals are used by the KGB to obtain assessment information on possible recruitment targets among the American personnel (those with money, family, drinking, or drug problems). The Soviets strictly limit the use of

Volunteers

local hires in their own Embassies, apparently concerned that if they can succeed, so can U.S. intelligence.

Third countries are commonly used by the Soviets as meeting places with recruited agents. Vienna, Austria, for example, was used as the meeting place for John Walker, who was convicted of spying for the Soviets.

Both as a command structure and as part of each member country's governmental structure, NATO is a high-priority target of the Soviet Union and other Warsaw Pact countries. These intelligence services place a very high priority on the recruitment of human assets with all levels of access to NATO and classified information; based on what is known of Soviet modus operandi in general, it is also presumed that a similar effort is made to effect physical penetration of NATO installations wherever they exist. Recent arrests in West Germany and Greece are indicative of the successes the USSR is having in targeting U.S. and NATO classified weapons systems.

The Chin case is an example of one of the PRC intelligence services' recruitment techniques. Chin, who admitted to passing classified information to his PRC contacts, operated in-place for a very long time following his recruitment as an agent. He admitted to suggesting a recruitment approach to another ethnic Chinese CIA employee. To use a recruited agent as a talent spotter of other potential agents among his peers is a standard intelligence practice employed by most intelligence services.

Appendix 2
ESPIONAGE ARRESTS AND PROSECUTIONS

Name	Arrest Date and Location	Conviction Date
Michael Timothy Tobias Navy	8/22/84 San Francisco, CA	8/14/85
Francis Xavier Pizzo Navy	8/22/84 San Francisco, CA	8/6/85
Bruce Edward Tobias Navy	8/23/84 San Diego, CA	1//22/85*
Dale Verne Irene Friend of Tobias	8/23/84 San Diego, CA	1/22/85
Alice Michelson KGB co-optee	10/1/84 New York, NY	5/31/85
Samuel Loring Morison Navy Analyst	10/1/84 Baltimore, MD	10/17/85
Richard W. Miller FBI Agent	10/2/84 Los Angeles, CA	6/19/86
Svetlana Ogorodnikova Soviet Consulate	10/2/84 Los Angeles, CA	6/25/85
Nikolay Ogorodnikova Soviet Consulate	10/2/84 Los Angeles, CA	6/26/85
Karel Frantisek Koecher Czechoslovakian Intel	11/27/84 New York, NY	2/3/86
Jay Clyde Wolff Former Navy	12/15/84 Albuquerque, NM	5/17/85
Thomas Patrick Cavanaugh Northrup Corporation	12/18/84 Los Angeles, CA	3/14/85
John Anthony Walker, Jr Former Navy	5/20/85 Baltimore, MD	10/28/85
Michael Lance Walker Navy	5/22/85 Aboard USS Nimitz Haifa, Israel	10/28/85
Arthur James Walker Former Navy	5/29/85 Norfolk, VA	8/9/85
Jerry Alfred Whitworth Former Navy	6/3/85 San Francisco, CA	7/24/86
Sharon Marie Scranage CIA Operations Support	7/11/85 Springfield, VA	9/27/85
Michael Agboutui Soussoudis Ghanian Intelligence	7/10/85 Springfield, VA	11/25/85
Jonathan Jay Pollard Navy Intelligence Analyst	11/21/85 Washington, DC	6/4/86
Anne Louise Pollard Wife of Jay	11/22/85 Washington, DC	6/4/86
Lawrence Wu-Tai Chin CIA Analyst	11/22/85 Alexandria, VA	2/7/86
Ronald William Pelton NSA Computer Specialist	11/25/85 Washington, DC	6/5/86
Randy Miles Jeffries Congressional Courier	12/20/85 Washington, DC	1/23/86
Bruce Damian Ott Air Force	1/22/86 Davis, CA	8/7/86
Gennadiy Fedorovich Zakharov KGB	8/23/86 New York, NY	9/30/86
Allen John Davies Former Air Force	10/27/86 San Francisco, CA	5/28/87

* Convicted of nonespionage charges (Theft of Government Statute).

Appendix 3[147]

DOD PERSONNEL ARRESTED OF ESPIONAGE

The following is a list of Department of Defense military and civilian employees arrested for espionage since the conclusion of World War II. Although not all-inclusive (because of the Privacy Act or classification), this list highlights the person's name, organization, and the foreign intelligence service the traitor was involved with. In some cases it was not known whether the KGB or the GRU was involved and in those cases SIS will be reflected. Air Force personnel (except for Butkeno who was not in the USAF or a civilian employee of the DAF; he worked for a firm which administered USAF contracts) are not included as their cases have already been extensively discussed in this study.

Appendix 3
DoD PERSONNEL INVOLVED IN ESPIONAGE

Name	Assignment	Foreign Intelligence Service
Attardi, Joseph	Army	Unknown
Baba, Stephan	Navy	South Africa
Bell, Williams	Hughes Aircraft	Polish
Butenko, John	Contractor	KGB
Cavanaugh, Thomas	Northrup	SIS
Cordrey, Robert E.	Marine	Note 1
Dedyan, Sahag K.	Johns Hopkins University	SIS
Drummond, Nelson	Navy	SIS
Dubberstein, Waldo H.	DIA	Libya
Dunlap, Jack	Army	KGB
Gessner, George J.	Army	SIS
Harper, James D.	Civilian	Polish
Harris, Ulysses L.	Army	SIS
Helmich, Joseph	Army	KGB
Horton, Brian P.	Navy	SIS
Humphrey, Ronald L.	U.S. Information Service	Vietnam
Johnson, Robert L.	Army	KGB
Ledbettor, Gary L.	Navy	SIS
Madsen, Lee E.	Navy	N/A
Mintkenbaugh, James	Army	KGB
Payne, Leslie J.	Army	East German
Rhodes, Roy Adir	Army	KGB
Rogalsky, Ivan	Civilian	SIS
Safford, Leonard J.	Army	SIS
Whalen, William H.	Army	SIS

Note 1: Cordrey attempted to contact the Soviets, East Germans, Polish and Czechoslovakian Intelligence Services

Appendix 4[148]

The following list highlights the motivation and prison sentence of Department of Defense military and civilian personnel arrested for espionage since the conclusion of World War II. The prison sentence reflected is the one initially imposed and does not reflect any reduction resulting from plea bargins, appeals, and so forth.

Appendix 4
ESPIONAGE MOTIVES OF DoD PERSONNEL

Name	Motivation	Sentence
Attardi	Unknown	3 Years
Baba	Money	8 Years
Bell	Money	8 Years
Butenko	Ideology	30 Years
Cavanaugh	Money	Life
Cordrey	Money	12 Years
Dedyan	Family Ties	3 Years
Drummond	Money	Life
Dubberstein	Possibly Money	Suicide
Dunlap	Money	Suicide
Gessner	Disgruntled	20 Years
Harper	Money	Life
Harris	Money	7 Years
Helmich	Money	Life
Horton	Money	6 Years
Humphrey	Family Ties	15 Years
Johnson	Money/Disgruntled	25 Years, Note 1
Ledbettor	Money	6 Months
Madsen	Money/Ego	8 Years
Mintkenbaugh	Revenge	25 Years
Payne	Possibly Money	4 Years
Rhodes	Blackmail	5 Years
Rogalsky	Possibly Money	Note 2
Safford	Money	25 Years
Whalen	Money	15 Years

Note 1: In 1972, Johnson was stabbed to death in his prison cell by his son.

Note 2: Rogalsky was deemed to be psychologically incompetent to stand trial. He had attempted to acquire data concerning the Space Shuttle Program from an RCA engineer.

ENDNOTES

Chapter 1

1. Sun Tzu, *The Art of War*, Chapter 4, "The Use of Secret Agents," edited by Samuel Griffith, Oxford University Press.

2. Ibid.

3. Haswell, Jock, *Spies and Spymasters: A Concise History of Intelligence*, Thames and Hudson, 1977, p. 8.

4. Sayle, Edward F., *The Historical Underpinnings of the U.S. Intelligence Community*, Defense Intelligence College, 1985, p. 8.

5. *Microdot Briefing Guide*, HQ Air Force Office of Special Investigations, Washington, D.C., 1986, p. 1.

6. Pincher, Chapman, *Too Secret Too Long*, St Martins Press, 1984, p. 34. Also see: Robert J. Lamphere and Tom Shachtman, *The FBI - KGB War: A Special Agent's Story*, Random House, pp. 78 - 98 and Viktor Suvorov, *Inside Soviet Military Intelligence*, MacMillan Publishing Company, 1984, p. 123.

7. Suvorov, Viktor, *Inside Soviet Military Intelligence*, MacMillan Publishing Company, New York, 1984, p. 123.

Chapter 2

1. AFOSI Investigative File, Subject: *Robert Glenn Thompson*, HQ Air Force Office of Special Investigations, Washington, DC, 1964.

2. *Saturday Evening Post*, May 22, 1965, p. 24.

3. Interview with SA Robert Miglia, HQ AFOSI Western Hemisphere Branch, Operations Division.

Endnotes

4   AFOSI Investigative File, Subject: Raymond George DeChamplain, HQ Air Force Office of Special Investigations, Washington, DC, 1971.

5   AFOSI Investigative File, Subject: Walter T. Perkins, HQ Air Force Office of Special Investigations, Washington, DC, 1971. This could have been disinformation on the Soviet's part to keep their agents motivated.

6   Ibid.

7   Interview on February 23, 1987, with Colonel Richard Law, Commander, AFOSI District 70, Lindsey AS, Germany and formerly AFOSI Director of Counterintelligence. Colonel Law interviewed Perkins extensively on several occasions and believes that Perkins claim of blackmail is plausible.

8   AFOSI Investigative File, re: Perkins. After all, Perkins was a career intelligence officer.

9   AFOSI Investigative File, Subject: Joseph Patrick Kauffman, HQ Air Force Office of Special Investigations, Washington, DC, 1961. The defector believed Kauffman would eventually ask for money if he had not been arrested. The defector believes that Kauffman did not want to appear greedy.

10 Barron, John, KGB: The Secret Work of Soviet Secret Agents, Corgi Books, London, 1974, p. 454.

11 Defense Science and Electronics, "Too Tall Ivan," Campbell, California, December 1987, p. 33.

12 Suvorov, Inside Soviet Military Intelligence, pp. 107-08. Also see: Crawford, David J., Paddy Bear: An Analysis of a Successful Double Agent Operation, HQ Air Force Office of Special Investigations, Washington, DC, 1986.

13 Suvorov, Inside Soviet Military Intelligence, p. 109.

14 Lecture presented to AFOSI Counterintelligence Investigations Class 87-A, Bolling AFB, Washington, DC, February 1986.

Volunteers

15 Kahn, David, <u>Hitlers Spies</u>, Macmillan, New York, p. 275.

16 Kessler, Ronald, <u>Regardie's</u>, "The Spy Game," November, 1986, p.99.

17 Suvorov, <u>Inside Soviet Military Intelligence</u>, p. 108.

18 <u>Tainik: An Analysis of Soviet Intelligence Service Dead Drop Activity in the United States 1976-1986</u>.

Chapter 3

1 Barron, John, <u>KGB Today: The Hidden Hand</u>, Hodder and Stoughton, London, 1983, p. 452. Barron notes that in the KGB, Department 14 is responsible for developing and supplying the technical tools for clandestine operations, to include concealment devices, self-destruct containers for transporting secret documents and film, disguised audio and radio equipment, cameras, and secret writing.

2 Haswell, Jock, <u>Spies and Spymasters: A Concise History of Intelligence</u>, Thames and Hudson Publishing, London, 1977, p. 8. The nickel in question was used to conceal microfilm. Unfortunately, over the years, a myth has been created that this nickel led directly to the detection and arrest of Rudolf Abel. The nickel was actually discovered several years before the Abel arrest and was mistakenly used by a member of Abel's agent network. The hollowed-out nickel made good print in the newspapers at the time and the myth continues today.

3 Crawford, David J., <u>Soviet and Warsaw Pact Concealment Devices and Espionage Cameras</u>, HQ Air Force Office of Special Investigations, Washington, DC, 1986, p. 1.

4 AFOSI Investigative Case File, Subject: <u>Bronson</u> HQ Air Force Office of Special Investigations, Washington, DC, 1979.

5 Thompson, Robert Glenn, "I Spied for the Russians," <u>The Saturday Evening Post</u>, New York, May 22, 1965, p. 29.

Endnotes

6   Thompson, Robert Glenn, "I Spied for the Russians," The Saturday Evening Post, New York, June 5, 1965, p. 40.

7   Suvorov, Viktor, Inside Soviet Military Intelligence, Macmillan Publishing Company, New York, 1984, p. 119.

8   Suvorov, p. 119.

9   Crawford, David J., Analysis of Soviet Intelligence Dead Drop Activity in the United States 1975 - 1986, HQ Air Force Office of Special Investigations, Washington, D.C., 1986, p. 1. Also see Breaking the Ring by John Barron and "The Spy Game" (Regardies) by Ronald Kessler.

10 Ibid.

11 Investigative Case File, re: Bronson

12 Suvorov, p. 124. One thing to remember when evaluating information from a defector is that the defector will only be able to describe the practices he has seen or heard about. Although KGB and GRU policy and tradecraft practices are standardized, as in any organization, different units located around the world may make deviations from normal practices.

13 Investigative Case File, re: Thompson. For a good description of how the dead drop and signal system works, refer to, Family Treason: The Walker Spy Case, Chapter 9, "Operation Windflyer." Kneece, the author, provides an unclassified description of how the Soviets communicated with Navy spy John Walker for more than 20 years. Walker had received dead drop and signal sites, maps, and photographs of the locations, and specific instructions to follow to avoid detection by surveillance and to allow the Soviets to conduct countersurveillance. Although Walker was observed at the dead drop locations and signal sites, the FBI was unable to detain the Soviet intelligence officer because he never went to the drop location. An FBI agent had removed the signal Walker had left and because he was unable to see the signal, the Soviet officer departed the area.

Volunteers

14   AFOSI Investigative Case File, Subject: <u>Herbert Boeckenhaupt</u>, HQ Air Force Office of Special Investigations, Washington, DC, 1965.

15   Ibid.

16   Ibid.

17   Cassidy, William L., <u>Clandestine Tactics and Technology: Studies in Tradecraft</u>, Bureau of Operations and Research, International Association of Police, Washington, DC, 1981, p. 16.

18   Ibid.

19   <u>Espionage, Treason and Sedition (Mutiny) Investigations</u>, HQ Air Force Office of Special Investigations Regulation 124-72, Washington, DC, 1982, p. A1-1.

20   Yost, Graham, <u>Spy - Tech</u>, Facts on File Publications, 1985, p. 212.

21   Cassidy, p. 14.

22   Thompson, <u>The Saturday Evening Post</u>, June 5, 1965, p. 38.

23   Ibid.

24   <u>Espionage, Treason and Mutiny Investigations</u>, A1-4.

25   <u>Microdot Briefing Guide</u>.

26   Yost, p. 214.

27   <u>Microdot Briefing Guide</u>, p. 1.

28   Ibid.

29   Ibid.

30   Yost, p. 214.

31   Thompson, June 5, 1965, p. 40.

Endnotes

32 *Espionage, Treason and Mutiny Investigations*, A1-7.

33 Suvorov, p. 123.

34 Thompson, 5 June 1965, p. 40.

35 *Soviet and Warsaw Pact Concealment Devices and Espionage Cameras*, p. 15. For a more detailed description, sketch, and photographs of rollover cameras, reference should be made to *AFOSIR 124-72* and *Soviet and Warsaw Pact Concealment Devices and Espionage Cameras*.

36 Thompson, May 22, 1965, p. 29.

37 AFOSI Investigative Case File, Subject: *Raymond DeChamplain*, HQ Air Force Office of Special Investigations, Washington, DC, 1971.

38 AFOSI Investigative Case File, *re: Bronson*.

39 AFOSI Investigative Case File, Subject: *Francisco de Asia Mira*, HQ Air Force Office of Special Investigations, Washington, DC, 1983.

40 Investigative Case File, *re: Bockenhaupt*.

Chapter 4

1 Glaser, Daniel, *Social Deviance*, University of Southern California, 1971, p. 46.

2 *The Sentinel of Freedom*, The Amercian People and the Defense of the Nations Secrets, U.S. Dept of Justice (FBI), Apr 87, p. 10.

3 "Greed Gains Ground," U.S. News and World Report, Jan. 25, 88, p. 10. See *Conspiracy of Silence: The Secret Life of Anthony Blunt* by Barrie Penrose and Simon Freeman for a discussion of Soviet intelligence practices concerning payment to ideological and intellectual agents. For example, they note that Elizabeth Bently, an American Communist and government

Volunteers

    employee in the 1930's had been offered a fur coat and air conditioner, and on another occasion was offered cash. She found the offer insulting because of her ideological belief as her motivation to commit espionage. Penrose and Freeman note that there is no conclusive evidence that the Soviets offered money to the British intellectual spies of the 1930's, 40's or 50's.

4   Brown, Brock, "Spyings Dirty Little Secret," Money, July 1987, p. 130. There are two reasons why USAF traitors have not received much money. First, many were detected early and had not fully established themselves as espionage agents. Second, it is only in the past few years that the Soviets have been willing to expend large sums of money to acquire information.

5   "Espionage: The Sergeants Revenge," Newsweek, Nov. 14, 1966, p. 37.

6   Patterns and Trends in Espionage, HQ Air Force Office of Special Investigations, Washington, DC, 1975.

Chapter 5

1   AFOSI Investigative Case File, Subject: Ahadi (Pseudonym), HQ Air Force Office of Special Investigations, Washington, DC, 1968.

2   Ibid.

3   Ibid.

4   Ibid.

5   "Espionage: The Sergeant's Revenge," Newsweek. Nov. 14, 1966, p. 31.

6   AFOSI Investigative Case File, Subject: Herbert W. Boeckenhaupt, HQ Air Force Office of Special Investigations, Washington, DC, 1965.

Endnotes

7   Ibid.

8   Ibid.

9   Ibid.

10 Ibid.

11 Time, Nov. 11, 1966, p. 33.

12 The New York Times, June 8, 1967, p. 3.

13 "American Found Guilty of Espionage," Stars and Stripes, May 8, 1962.

14 Military Personnel Records, re: Borger.

15 Ibid.

16 Scott, Herb, "Germany to Try US Citizen as Agent for Reds," Stars and Stripes, April 29, 1962.

17 Ibid.

18 Stars and Stripes, May 8, 1962.

19 Ibid.

20 Ibid.

21 Interview with Lt Col Scott Schrader on Dec. 9, 1986. (He is presently the AFOSI Detachment Commander at Clark AFB, Republic of the Philippines.) Lt Col Schrader was awarded the National Intelligence Medal for his work during this investigation.

22 AFOSI Investigative Case File, re: Bronson.

23 Ibid.

24 Interview with Lt Col Schrader.

Volunteers

25 Ibid.

26 Ibid.

27 Ibid.

28 Ibid.

29 AFOSI Investigative Case File, re: Bronson.

30 Interview with Lt Col Schrader.

31 AFOSI Investigative Case File, Subject: Edward Owen Buchanan, Statement of Source, AF Form 1169/70, May 9, 1985.

32 AFOSI Investigative Case File, re: Buchanan, Statement of Source, AF Form 1169/70, May 10, 1985.

33 AFOSI Investigative Case File, re: Buchanan, Statement of Subject, AFOSI Form 73, May 17, 1985 and agents investigative notes.

34 AFOSI Investigative Case File, re: Buchanan, Congressional Inquiry, 22 July 85, File Number 5793220011.

35 Ibid. Buchanan believed that a discharge from the United States Air Force would stop all legal proceedings against him.

36 "Air Force Says Fast Investigative Work Saved Sabre Secrets," The New York Times, Nov. 26, 1952, p. 9.

37 "Aid to the Enemy," Newsweek, Dec. 8, 1952, p. 44.

38 "US Airman Held in Korean Spy Plot," The New York Times, Nov. 25, 1952, p. 6.

39 "Sergeant Gets 20 Years on Jet Conspiracy Charge," The New York Times, June 9, 1953, p. 7.

40 Reese, Michael, Shannon, Elaine, Martin, David, and Lord Mary. "The Strange Case of Christopher Cooke," Newsweek, May 1982, p. 3. Lt Cooke advised during his interview with AFOSI investigators that he called his parents, advised them he was calling from the Library of Congress and would be home late because his car had broken down.

41 AFOSI Investigative Case File, Subject: Christopher M. Cooke, HQ Air Force Office of Special Investigations, Bolling AFB, Washington, DC, 1981.

42 Ibid.

43 Ibid.

44 Ibid.

45 Ibid.

46 Ibid.

47 Ibid.

48 Interview in April 1987 with Mr. Charles R. Torpy, AFOSI Assistant For National Programs, who was Director of Counterintelligence at the time of the Cooke investigation.

49 Ibid.

50 Ibid.

51 Interview on February 23, 1987 with Special Agent Dan Bruno (currently assigned to HQ AFOSI, Directorate of Counterintelligence, Operations Division, as the Chief of the Research and Training Programs Branch) who worked on the investigation and interviewed Crest.

52 Ibid.

53 Ibid.

54 AFOSI Investigative Case File, Subject: Crest (pseudonym), HQ Air Force Office of Special Investigations, Washington, DC, 1976.

Volunteers

55 Ibid.

56 Interview with Mr. Bruno.

57 Ibid.

58 Ibid.

59 AFOSI Investigative Case File, re: **Crest**.

60 Thornton, Mary, "FBI Arrest Ex-Airman on Espionage Charges," The Washington Post, Oct. 28, 1986, p. A21.

61 Ibid.

62 Ibid.

63 Wright, Stephen E., "Spy Suspect Cites Revenge," San Jose Mercury News, Jan. 7, 1987, p. 1.

64 AFOSI Investigative Case File, Subject: **John Allen Davies**, HQ Air Force Office of Special Investigations, Washington, DC, 1986.

65 Gertz, Bill, "Technician In Silicon Valley Charged by FBI Counterspies," The Washington Times, Oct. 28, 1986, p. 3A.

66 AFOSI Investigative Case File, Subject: **Raymond George DeChamplain**, HQ Air Force Office of Special Investigations, Washington, DC, 1971.

67 "GI Held For Helping Communist Spies," Bangkok Post, July 25, 1971.

68 Investigative case file, re: **DeChamplain**.

69 Ibid.

70 "Sergeant Tried On Espionage Charges," The Washington Daily News, Nov. 2, 1971.

71 "US Officer Gets Life for Spying," New York Herald Tribune, September 23, 1957.

Endnotes

72 "US Flier Guilty of Spy Attempt," The New York Times, Sep. 22, 1957.

73 Ibid.

74 "The Strange Case of Bombardier French," U.S. News and World Report, Oct. 4, 1957.

75 "Atom Secret Sale Verdict is Upheld," The Washington Post, Feb. 7, 1959.

76 "Davis-Monthan Jury Again Convicts Airman of U-2 Data Offer," Arizona Daily Star, June 18, 1977.

77 Wippman, Lawrence, "Airman Loses Espionage Appeal," Tucson Citizen, June 17, 1977.

78 "Davis-Monthan Jury Again Convicts..."

79 "Airman Loses Espionage Appeal."

80 AFOSI Investigative Case File, Subject: Herman (pseudonym), HQ Air Force Office of Special Investigations, Washington, DC, 1967.

81 Ibid.

82 Ibid.

83 "U.S. Airman is Held in Korean Spy Plot," The New York Times, Nov. 25, 1952, p. 1.

84 AFOSI Investigative Case File, Subject: Joseph Patrick Kauffman, HQ Air Force Office of Special Investigations, Washington, DC, 1961.

85 Interview with Brigadier General Richard S. Beyea, Jr., Commander, Air Force Office of Special Investigations, on March 31, 1987.

86 Ibid.

87 Ibid.

88 Ibid.

Volunteers

89   Ibid.

90   AFOSI Investigative Case File, Subject: <u>Francisco De Asis Mira</u>, HQ Air Force Office of Special Investigations, Washington, DC, 1983.

91   Briefing script, <u>The Mira Case</u>, HQ Air Force Office of Special Investigations, Bolling AFB, Washington, DC.

92   Ibid.

93   Investigative case file, re: **Mira**

94   Interview in March 1987 with Special Agent Al Huff (presently assigned to AFOSI District 21, Langley AFB, Va) who worked on the Mira investigation and participated in his interviews.

95   Ibid.

96   Hodgson, Dick, "Airman is Sentenced for Spy Activities," <u>The Stars and Stripes</u>, Aug. 29, 1984, p. 1.

97   Fanning, Win, "Agents Say Cpl Sought To Aid Russia," <u>Stars and Stripes</u>, Apr. 15, 1950, Garmisch, Germany.

98   Ibid. Mueller's mother vehemently denied this.

99   Ibid.

100 Fanning, Win, "Mueller Guilty-Gets 5 Years," <u>Stars and Stripes</u>, April 16, 1950, Garmisch, Germany. Army psychologists described Mueller as "immature and emotionally unstable."

101 Glover, Mark, "Sale of Spy Data Filmed," <u>Sacramento Bee</u>, July 26, 1986.

102 Ibid.

103 Bunstein, Daniel, "Accused Beale Spy Told He Can't Skip Trial, <u>Sacramento Bee</u>, July 23, 1986.

104 "Ott Allegedly Admitted Spy Attempt," <u>Fairfield Daily Republic</u>, Aug. 5, 1986 and also AFOSI Investigative Case File.

Endnotes

105 "Airman Ott Found Guilty of Selling SR-71 Secrets," Fairfield Daily Republic, August 7, 1986.

106 Bunstein.

107 AFOSI Investigative Case File, re: Ott.

108 Kell, Gretchen, "Graduation Called Turning Point For Spy Suspect," Sacramento Bee, July 30, 1986.

109 Information provided by Major Richard Certo, Chief, Counterintelligence Division, AFOSI District 19, Travis, AFB, California.

110 Kell, Gretchen, "Prison Term in Spy Case: Beale Airman Gets 25 Years," Sacramento Bee, Aug. 8, 1986.

111 _____. "Airman Convicted in Spy Case," Sacramento Bee, August 1986, p. 1.

112 Barron, John, KGB: The Secret Work of Soviet Secret Agents, Corgi Books, London, 1974, p. 3.

113 AFOSI Investigative Case File, Subject: Walter T. Perkins, HQ Air Force Office of Special Investigations, Washington, DC, 1971.

114 Ibid.

115 AFOSI Investigative Case File, re: Perkins, Preliminary Damage Assessment Report, April 12, 1972.

116 AFOSI Investigative Case File, re: Perkins

117 Ibid.

118 Colonel Richard Law, Commander, AFOSI District 70, Lindsey AS, Germany, and formerly AFOSI Director of Counterintelligence. Colonel Law interviewed Perkins extensively on several occasions and believes that Perkins claim of blackmail is reasonably accurate. Interview with Colonel Law on February 23, 1986.

Volunteers

119   Ibid.

120   AFOSI Investigative Case File, <u>Sentinel Score Questionare</u>, completed by Perkins on February 26, 1968, when he was requesting a transfer back to HUMINT duties.

121   AFOSI Investigative Case File, re: <u>Perkins</u>.

122   AFOSI Investigative Case File, Subject: <u>Robert Glenn Thompson</u>, HQ Air Force Office of Special Investigations, Washington, DC, 1964.

123   Ibid.

124   Thompson, Robert Glenn, "I Spied For the Russians," <u>The Saturday Evening Post</u>, May 22, 1965, p. 25.

125   AFOSI Investigative Case File, re: <u>Thompson</u>.

126   Ibid.

127   Thompson, "I Spied For the Russians," May 22, 1965, p. 29.

128   Ibid.

129   Thompson, Robert Glenn, "I Spied For the Russians (Part II)," <u>The Saturday Evening Post</u>, June 5, 1965, p. 39.

130   Ibid, p. 42.

131   Ibid.

132   Ibid, p. 44.

133   AFOSI Investigative Case File, re: <u>Thompson</u>.

134   Ibid.

135   AFOSI Investigative Case File, Subject: <u>Walton</u> (pseudonym), HQ Air Force Office of Special Investigations, Washington, DC, 1982.

136   Ibid.

Endnotes

137 AFOSI Investigative Case File, Subject: <u>Wesson</u> (pseudonym), HQ Air Force Office of Special Investigations, Washington, DC, 1984.

138 Ibid.

139 AFOSI Investigative Case File, Subject: <u>James David Wood</u>, HQ Air Force Office of Special Investigations, Washington, DC, 1973.

140 <u>Washington-Star News</u>, "Russian Named in Spy Case," Aug. 22, 1973. According to the FBI affidavit, Wood carried a letter with directions to make the rendevous. He was to wear a blue sports jacket with a copy of <u>Time</u> magazine sticking out from the right side pocket. Wood complained that the Soviet instructions "were pretty damned ignorant."

141 Investigative Case File, re: <u>Wood</u>.

142 Ibid.

143 Ibid.

144 Ibid.

145 Ibid.

146 Ibid.

147 Jepson, Larry, <u>Espionage Directed Against U.S. Military Interests Since World War II</u>, Defense Intelligence College, Washington, DC, 1987.

148 Ibid.

BIBLIOGRAPHY

AFOSI Special Report: Profiles In Espionage - Seven Case Studies HQ Air Force Office of Special Investigations, Washington, DC, July 1976.

Andrew, Christopher, Her Majesty's Secret Service, Viking Press, New York, 1986.

Arizona Daily Star, "Davis-Monthan Jury Again Convicts Airman of U-2 Data Offer," Tucson, Arizona, June 18, 1977.

Bangkok Post, "GI Held For Helping Communist Spies," July 25, 1971.

_____. "Accused Spy had Financial Problems," July 28, 1971.

Barron, John, KGB: The Secret Work of Soviet Secret Agents, Corgi Books, London, 1975.

_____. KGB Today: The Hidden Hand, Hodder and Stoughton, London, 1983.

_____. Breaking the Ring: The Bizzare Case of the Walker Family Spy Ring, Houghton-Miflin Company, Boston, 1987.

Beecher, William, International Herald Tribune, "GI Seized as Spy Reportedly Set Trip to Free Russians," October 23-24, 1971.

Bennett, George F., Burlington County Times, "Spy Trial Postponed Till December 3," Burlington County, New Jersey, November 7, 1973.

_____. Burlington County Times, "Sgt to Plead Innocent to Charges of Spying," Burlington County, New Jersey, November 6, 1973.

Blair, W. Granger, New York Times, "Briton Accused in Security Case," November 2, 1966.

Bledowska, Celina and Bloch, Jonathan, KGB - CIA Intelligence and Counterintelligence Operations, Bison Books, London, 1987.

Brown, Brock, "Spyings Dirty Little Secret," Money, July 1987.

Bibliography

Buckley, Mike, "Disbelief Over Spy Charges," *Seattle Post-Intelligence*, August 27, 1973.

Bunstein, Daniel, "Accused Beale Spy Told He Can't Skip Trial," *Sacramento Bee*, Sacramento, California, July 23, 1986.

Cassidy, William L., *Clandestine Tactics and Technology: Studies in Tradecraft*, Bureau of Operations and Research, International Association of Police, Washington, DC, 1981.

Contra Costa Times, "Roll of the Dice: Psychiatrist Testifies in Spy Trial," Contra Costa, California, July 30, 1986.

Corson, William R. and Crowley, Robert T., *The New KGB: Engine of Soviet Power*, William Morrow and Company, New York, 1985.

Crawford, David J., *Analysis of Soviet Intelligence Dead Drop Activity in the United States 1975 - 1986*, HQ Air Force Office of Special Investigations, 1986.

_____. *Soviet and Warsaw Pact Intelligence Services Concealment Devices and Espionage Cameras*, HQ Air Force Office of Special Investigations, Washington, DC, 1986.

_____. *Soviet Short Range Agent Communication*, HQ Air Force Office of Special Investigations, Washington, DC, 1986.

_____. *Espionage Against the Air Force: The Ott and Buchanan Cases*, HQ Air Force Office of Special Investigations, Washington, DC, 1986.

_____. *Espionage In the Air Force Since World War II*, HQ Air Force Office of Special Investigations, Washington, DC, 1987.

Daily Press, "Soviet Embassy Visit Forced Missile Changes," Newport News, Virginia, June 1, 1981.

Daily Republic, "Ott Allegedly Admitted Spy Attempt," Sacramento, California, August 5, 1986.

Deacon, Richard, *Kempei Tai: A History of the Japanese Secret Service*, Berkley Books, New York, 1985.

Volunteers

_____. *The Israeli Secret Service*, Taplinger Publishing Company, New York, 1977.

_____. *A History of the Russian Secret Service*, Grafton Books, London, 1987.

_____. *A History of the British Secret Service*, Granada Publishing, London, 1984.

Defense Science and Electronics, "Too Tall Ivan," December 1987.

Department of the Air Force, *Legislative Liaison Digest*, Volume 119, 128, September 6, 1973.

Dziak, John, *Chekisty*, Lexington Books, Boston, 1988.

Espionage, Treason and Mutiny Investigations, HQ Air Force Office of Special Investigations Regulation (AFOSIR 124-72), Washington, DC, 1982.

Fairfield Daily Republic, "Airman Ott Found Guilty of Selling SR-71 Secrets," Fairfield, California, August 7, 1986.

Gertz, Bill, "Technician In Silicon Valley Charged by FBI Counterspies," *The Washington Times*, October 28, 1986.

Godson, Roy, *Intelligence Requirements for the 1980's: Counterintelligence*, National Strategy Information Center, Washington, DC, 1980.

Glasser, Daniel, *Social Deviance*, University of Southern California, 1971.

Glees, Anthony, *The Secrets of the Service*, Carrol and Graf Publishers, New York 1987.

Glover, Mark, *Sacramento Bee*, "Sale of Spy Data Filmed," Sacramento, California, July 26, 1986.

Griffith, Samuel B., *Sun Tzu - The Art of War* (translated and edited), Oxford University Press, London, 1963.

Graham, Fred P., *The New York Times*, Oct. 31, 1966.

Halloran, Richard, *The New York Times*, "Officer Said To Have Given Data Titan To Russians," June 1, 1981.

Bibliography

Haswell, Jock, <u>Spies and Spymasters: A Concise History of Intelligence</u>, Thames and Hudson Publishing, London, 1977.

Hinsley, F.H., <u>British Intelligence In the Second World War</u>, Volumes 1 - 3, H.M. Stationary Office, London, 1981.

Hodgson, Dick, <u>Stars and Stripes</u>, "Airman is Sentenced for Spy Attempt," August 29, 1984.

Havourd, Russ, "State Man will Stand Trial in Guam on Espionage Counts," <u>Hartford Courant</u>, July 28, 1971.

Investigative Case File, <u>Subject: Ahadi</u> (pseudonym), HQ Air Force Office of Special Investigations, Washington, DC, 1967.

Investigative Case File, <u>Subject: Herbert Boeckenhaupt</u>, HQ Air Force Office of Special Investigations, Washington, DC, 1965.

Investigative Case File, <u>Subject: Bronson</u> (pseudonym), HQ Air Force Office of Special Investigations, Washington, DC, 1980.

Investigative Case File, <u>Subject: Edward Buchanan</u>, HQ Air Force Office of Special Investigations, Washington, DC, 1985.

Investigative Case File, <u>Subject: Christopher Cooke</u>, HQ Air Force Office of Special Investigations, Washington, DC, 1981.

Investigative Case File, <u>Subject: Crest</u> (pseudonym), HQ Air Force Office of Special Investigations, Washington, DC, 1976.

Investigative Case File, <u>Subject: John Allen Davies</u>, HQ Air Force of Special Investigations, Washington, DC, 1986.

Investigative Case File, <u>Subject: Raymond DeChamplain</u>, HQ Air Force Office of Special Investigations, Washington, DC, 1971.

Investigative Case File, <u>Subject: George French</u>, HQ Air Force Office of Special Investigations, Washington, DC, 1957.

Volunteers

Investigative Case File, Subject: Oliver Grunden, HQ Air Force Office of Special Investigations, Washington, DC, 1973.

Investigative Case File, Subject: Herman (pseudonym), HQ Air Force Office of Special Investigations, Washington, DC, 1967.

Investigative Case File, Subject: Joseph Kauffman, HQ Air Force Office of Special Investigations, Washington, DC

Investigative Case File, Subject: Francisco De Asis Mira, HQ Air Force Office of Special Investigations, Washington, DC, 1983.

Investigative Case File, Subject: Bruce Ott, HQ Air Force Office of Special Investigations, Washington, DC, 1986.

Investigative Case File, Subject: Walter Perkins, HQ Air Force Office of Special Investigations, Washington, DC, 1971.

Investigative Case File, Subject: Robert Thompson, HQ Air Force Office of Special Investigations, Washington, DC, 1964.

Investigative Case File, Subject: Wesson (pseudonym), HQ Air Force Office of Special Investigations, Washington, DC, 1984.

Investigative Case File, Subject: Walton (pseudonym), HQ Air Force Office of Special Investigations, Washington, DC, 1982.

Investigative Case File, Subject: James Wood, HQ Air Force Office of Special Investigations, Washington, DC, 1973.

Jepson, Larry, Espionage Directed Against U.S. Military Interests Since World War II, Defense Intelligence College, Washington, DC, 1987.

Kell, Gretchen, Sacramento Bee, "Graduation Called Turning Point for Spy Suspect," Sacramento, California, July 30, 1986.

_____. Sacramento Bee, "Accused Spy Probably Sane, Doctors Testify," Sacramento, California, Aug. 5, 1986.

_____. Sacramento Bee, "Airman Convicted in Spy Case," August 7, 1986.

_____. Sacramento Bee, "Prison Term in Spy Case: Beale Airman Gets 25 Years," Sacramento, California, August 8, 1986.

Kessler, Ronald, Regardie's, "The Spy Game," Washington, DC, November 1986.

Kneece, Jack, Family Treason: The Walker Spy Case, Stein and Day Publishers, New York, 1986.

Knudson, Richard L., The Whole Spy Catalog, St. Martins Press, New York, 1986.

Knightly, Philip, The Second Oldest Profession, Knopf, New York, 1987.

Kornblum, Allan, Intelligence and The Law, Volumes I-VI, Defense Intelligence College, Washington, DC, 1987.

_____. The Counterintelligence Game, Volumes I-IV, Defense Intelligence College, Washington, DC, 1987.

Lamphere, Robert J. and Tom Shachtman, The FBI - KGB War: A Special Agents Story, Random House, New York, 1986.

Langholf, Deaver, and Crawford, David J. Secret Writing: A Historical and Operational Perspective, HQ Air Force Office of Special Investigations, Washington, DC, January 1988.

Laqueur, Walter, A World of Secrets, Basic Books, New York, 1985.

McCarthy, Michael, The Overseas Weekly Stateside, "AF Sgt Admits Spying For Russians," Vol. 28, No. 52, December 24, 1973.

Middletown Press, "Connecticut Air Force man Held on Espionage Charges," July 24, 1971.

Microdot Briefing Guide, HQ Air Force Office of Special Investigations, Washington, DC, 1986.

Volunteers

Murphy, Brendan M., Turncoat: The Strange Case of British Traitor Harold Cole, Harcourt Brace Jovanovich Publishers, New York, 1987.

New Haven Journal, "State GI to Stand Trial in Thailand Spy Case," September 21, 1971.

Newsweek, "Espionage: The Sergeant's Revenge," November 14, 1966.

_____. "Aid to the Enemy?", December 8, 1952.

New York Herald Tribune, "US Officer Get Life For Spying," September 23, 1957.

_____. "The Strange Case of Capt French," September 28, 1957.

The New York Times, "U.S. Airman is Held in Korean Spy Plot," November 25, 1952.

_____. "Accused Sergeant Held Mentally Ill," November 25, 1952.

_____. "Jet Spy Suspect Denies Guilt," June 3, 1952.

_____. "Sergeant Get 20 Years on Jet Conspiracy Charge," June 9, 1953.

_____. "Air Force Sergeant Held for Espionage for Aid to Russians," August 21, 1973.

Patterns and Trends in Espionage, HQ Air Force Office of Special Investigations, Washington, DC, 1975.

Penrose, Barrie and Freeman, Simon, Conspiracy of Silence: The Secret Life of Anthony Blunt, Grafton Books, London, 1987.

Pincher, Chapman, Too Secret Too Long, St Martins Press, London, 1984.

_____. Their Trade Is Treachery, Bantam Books, London, 1981

_____. Traitors: The Anatomy of Treason, St Martins Press, London 1987.

Bibliography

Radosh, Ronald and Milton, Joyce, The Rosenburg File, Holt, Rinehart Winston Publisher, New York, 1983.

Reese, Michael, Shannon, Elaine, Martin, David C. and Lord Mary, Newsweek, "The Strange Case of Christopher Cooke," New York, 1981.

Sayle, Edward F., The Historical Underpinnings of the U.S. Intelligence Community, Defense Intelligence College, Washington, DC, 1985.

Sacramento Bee, "Quiet and An Espionage Suspect," Sacramento, California, June 4, 1986.

Soviet Intelligence Services: The KGB and GRU, U.S. Government Publication, Washington, DC, 1984.

Suvorov, Viktor, Inside Soviet Military Intelligence, Macmillan Publishing Company, New York, 1984.

_____. Inside the Aquarium, Macmillan Publishing Company, New York, 1986.

Taylor, Henry J., Baltimore News American, "Red Spies in the U.S.," August 29, 1973.

The New York Times, "US Flier Guilty of Spy Attempt," September 22, 1957.

The Overseas Weekly - Stateside, "Lawyers Charge Secret Videotape Photos Taken," November 26, 1973.

The Secret War, Time Life Books, Chicago, 1981.

The Stars and Stripes, "Airman is Sentenced for Spy Activities," August 29, 1984.

Thompson, Robert Glenn, "I Spied for the Russians," The Saturday Evening Post, Philadelphia, 22 May and 5 June 1965.

Time, November 11, 1966.

_____. "The Garbage Collector," August 20, 1973.

Volunteers

Travis, Falcon; Hindley, Judy; Thomson, Ruth; Amery, Heather; Rawson, Christopher; and Harper, Anita, The Spy's Guidebook, Usborne Publishing Ltd, London, 1978.

Tucson Citizen, "Airman Loses Espionage Appeal," Tucson, Arizona, June 17, 1977.

U.S. Court of Military Appeals, Cooke V. Orser (et al), February 22, 1982.

_____. DeChamplain V. McLucas (et al), November 13, 1973.

U.S. News And World Report, "The Strange Case Of Bombardier French," October 4, 1957.

Washington Daily News, "Sergeant Tried on Espionage Charges," November 2, 1971.

Washington - Star News, "Sgt Cited For Espionage," Washington, DC, August 21, 1973.

_____."Sgt Charged with Treason," Washington, DC, August 20, 1973.

_____. "Russian Named in Spy Case," August 22, 1973.

The Washington Post, "Russian Diplomat In Spy Case Named," Washington, DC, August 22, 1973.

_____. "Atom Secret Sale Verdict Is Upheld," Washington, DC, February 7, 1959.

Washington Post Magazine, "Spy Rings of One," December 4, 1983.

West, Nigel, MI-5: British Security Service Operations 1909-1945, Stein and Day Publishers, New York, 1981.

_____. MI-5: 1945-1972 - A Matter of Trust, Weidenfeld and Nicolson, London, 1982.

_____. MI-6: British Secret Intelligence Service Operations 1909-1945, Weidenfeld and Nicolson, London, 1983.

Bibliography

_____. GCHG: The Secret Wireless War 1900-1986, Hodder and Stoughton, London, 1987.

Wilson, George C. International Herald Tribune, "Top NonCom at Weapons Base Held in U.S. in Security Case," Friday, October 22, 1971.

Wright, Stephen E., "Spy Suspect Cites Revenge, San Jose Mercury News, January 7, 1987.

Yost, Graham, Spy - Tech, Facts on File Publications, New York, 1985.

Yardley, Herbert O., "Secret Inks," The Saturday Evening Post, Philadelphia, April 4, 1931.

Zim, Herbert S., Codes and Secret Writing, Scholastic Book Services, New York, 1966.

Published by Books Express Publishing
Copyright © Books Express, 2010
ISBN 978-1-907521-12-6
To purchase copies at discounted prices please contact
info@books-express.com

The publishers have made every effort to contact the copyright holders of images 9, 10, 20 and 32 in this book. We would welcome correspondece from these companies/individuals that we have been unable to trace.